Pushing Through

My Journey of Weight Loss, Depression, Infertility & Suicidal Ideations

Charise Marie

Copyright ©2017 Charise Marie

All rights reserved. Without limiting the rights under copyright reserved above. No part of this book may be reproduced, stored in or introduced into a retrieval system, or transmitted in any form, or by any means (electronic, mechanical, photocopying, recording, or otherwise) without prior written consent from the author except brief quotes used in reviews, interviews, magazines or online. This is a work of non-fiction. It is not meant to depict, portray or represent any particular real person. Any references or similarities to actual events, entities, real people living or dead, or to real locations are intended for the sole purpose of giving this novel a sense of reality. Any similarities with other names, characters, entities, places, people or incidents are entirely coincidental.

ISBN: 0-9998459-1-8

ISBN-13: 978-0-9998459-1-2

Dedication

This book is dedicated to my children: My son Mr. J. & my daughter Ms. Z. and any future children I may have. Without you guys I wouldn't be who I am today and would not have been able to write this book. I love you guys to infinity times infinity and beyond. You both are the air that I breathe.

To my mom, my rock, my superwoman: I love you for everything that you have done for me, taught me and for never giving up on me.

Table Of Contents

Acknowledgements	i
Chapter One: A Star is Born!	1
Chapter Two: Baby Brown's Arrival	9
Chapter Three: Weight No More	25
Chapter Four: First Day of My New Life	36
Chapter Five: Starting Over	51
Chapter Six: Baby Fever	57
Chapter Seven: The Worse Day of My Life	67
Chapter Eight: Dust Yourself Off and Try Again	109
Chapter Nine: Unexpected	131
Chapter Ten: Disturbance	144
Chapter Eleven: The Storm	169
Chapter Twelve: After the Storm There's a Rainbow	205

Acknowledgements

I would like to thank all of my family, friends, associates and significant others that are referenced in this book. I appreciate you all for shaping and molding me into the woman that I am today.
Thank you for being a part of my story, my journey and my life.

Charise Marie
Chapter One:
A Star Is Born

January 1979

On a cold, snowy, Monday morning, on January 8th at 1:58 a.m., a big, beautiful, baby girl was born. She weighed eight pounds, nine ounces.

Yes, a star was born!

Well, at least my parents thought this was true when they saw me. A pleasantly plump baby girl I was. I looked like an Asian baby, or so I was told, but with extremely dark, curly hair. I had a light complexion and my eyes squinted some. I've heard the story of my birth numerous times over the years.

Around six to eight weeks old, I developed chicken pox. It left a permanent mark on the left side of my face that resembles a mole.

My mother had it rough with me as a child. I was diagnosed with breathing problems when I was young. It was discovered later that there were some bronchial problems I experienced during the first few years of my life. I had suffered so many chest infections and bouts of pneumonia by the time I was two years old that one doctor finally told my

Pushing Through

mom that I had asthma; severe asthma at that.

Around the age of four or five, I was intubated and rushed to the hospital because I had stopped breathing. Once I arrived in the emergency room by ambulance, the nurses pushed my mom out of the room. All mom saw was a huge needle and a lot of tubes and ventilators. They said I had stopped breathing twice for a few seconds, but with the grace of God and lots of prayers, they got me breathing again.

My mom said that she was scared to death. She said that she just kept praying to God: "Please don't take my baby girl, God, please don't take my baby girl."

Mom explained that I had tubes placed down my throat when I was around one year old, but it was nothing compared to the attack I had at four or five. They had to feed me by tube during this attack because of all the tubes running in and out of me.

Doctors have told my mom for years that I would grow out of it. She and I still pray today that I will grow out of having asthma.

I suffered from severe asthma for years and it was no fun. I was in and out of the hospital so often that the doctors and nurses knew my name before looking at my chart. Even when I was admitted for overnight stays, some of the nurses on the other floors knew exactly who I was.

My attacks resulted in me being in the hospital for up to seven days at a time. Sometimes the attacks were so bad

Charise Marie

that I'd be there for weeks. It didn't matter what I did, my asthma flared up: jump rope, run down the stairs, get overly excited, eat oranges. Yes, eat oranges.

My asthma would show up out of nowhere. There were so many triggers, including hot weather, snowy weather, very cold weather, the heat in the house being too high, or even the rugs at home.

The doctor's did a study on me in my early years on what made my asthma act up. The results? Mice droppings, pet dander, and certain types of rugs. It didn't matter what it was, my asthma seemed to take on a life of its own. I stayed out of breath nearly 90 percent of the time. My mom told me one day that she was told by a family friend to, "put me on a disability check." She said that she didn't want to put me on a monthly check for it would hinder me from knowing what it's like being out in the real world and working for money. She didn't want me to become lazy and think that lying around collecting a check was all I needed to be doing in life.

Some days I thought that if I just held my breath a little while longer, I wouldn't be so much for my mom to deal with. I even thought that things would be easier for my mom without me, so I stopped taking my medication. I tried a few times to take more than the prescribed dose of my inhaler just to see what it would do to me—it just made my head woozy and the room spin.

I was not severely overweight as a child, but I wasn't the average size either. My doctors usually said that I was around ten to fifteen pounds overweight, but that I wasn't

Pushing Through

obese. My weight didn't have a huge impact on my asthma. My asthma was just that, my asthma.

I was placed on steroids multiple times during my childhood. Steroids (I took Prednisone) were not my best friend when they had to be given to me with a needle, but steroids were my best friend in a sense. Taking them helped me breathe so much better. The only thing I hated about them, other than the needle, was that they made me want to continuously eat.

Weight gain is one of the biggest side effects of taking Prednisone. I remember when I was around twelve years old, my mom made dinner for the family. I ate a piece of steak, a pork chop, and an entire plate of collard greens and rice. That's when I knew steroids were not my friend. Typically, when I was admitted to the hospital, the doctors gave me a breathing treatment followed by a steroid shot. Although I dreaded getting that needle, those steroids helped me breathe better and faster every single time. Years later Prednisone changed from needle form to pill form. The steroid pill took more time to get through my system, though, so I would be in the hospital longer. However, I didn't like taking the pill because it left an awful taste in my mouth.

I thought my mom was trying to kill me one night after leaving the hospital. We were standing at the bus stop waiting to go home after I had an asthma attack. Suddenly, my mom told me to face her and she pushed me into her chest. I could not understand why she would tell me to put my face in her coat. Years later I understood that she was trying to shield me from the wind because it had been known to take my breath away.

Charise Marie

Around the time I turned nine years old and was leaving the fourth grade, my school announced that it was closing down for good. The teachers took everyone who attended the school skating at the local rink. I did not know how to skate, so my mom just told me to be careful.

While skating, my friends and I kept falling on our bottoms. We were kids so we laughed, got back up, dusted ourselves off, and tried again. The problem was that I tried one too many times.

My mom noticed about a week after the skating party that I was starting to limp. She asked me what was wrong, and I told her that my hip hurt really badly. She took me to the hospital and they told her I had a SCFE (pronounced skiffy).

She said, "A what?"

I had a Slipped Capital Femoral Epiphysis. The doctor explained that the ball in my hip was slipping off my hip joint and that I would need to have surgery. He let us know that the right hip was not that bad, but the left one was. He scheduled me for surgery mid-summer and told my mom that I would be out of school for a few months. He also told her that I would probably have a slight limp and arthritis for the rest of my life. We had just moved into a new home in a completely different neighborhood, but my grandparents were not happy about me being so far away. They wanted me there with them so they could take care of me.

My mom agreed to let me live with my grandparents because she was tired from running back and forth between

Pushing Through

work and my new school to get my homework. She was like Superwoman; at least, she was like my Superwoman.

She went to the school two or three times a week to get all my daily assignments, book reports, and homework. The teachers explained to my mom they believe I had dyslexia. Dyslexia is a learning disorder that affects your ability to read, spell, write, and speak. The one teacher explained to my mom that she just learns and understands things differently.

After the surgery, there was a checkup on my left hip, they noticed that the right hip was starting to slip as badly as the left one, so they scheduled surgery for the right hip and did that hip as not long after. I missed my entire fifth-grade year. I never stepped foot in my classroom. My Superwoman—my mom, with the help of my grandparents, ensured that I passed fifth grade. Mom homeschooled me with the materials she got from the school.

I was on crutches the last one to two months of school, and when I arrived, the kids had heard of my situation and knew that I was part of the class. I was able to graduate from a school I had barely attended.

In 1995 I experienced the worst kind of pain ever: my grandmother, my Nana, died. Her death hurt me very deeply. I had turned sixteen years old that year, had had a sweet-sixteen family dinner, and a party at my parents' home with friends. I also went to my junior prom.

Nana passed away November 9th, 1995, right before the holidays. It was very difficult for the family, and I think I

Charise Marie

took it extra hard. My grandmother— "Nana" was what everyone called her—was the true backbone of our family. She was funny, loving, caring, sweet, giving, a great cook, and just an all-around wonderful grandmother.

    She and my grandfather, Pop Pop, were the best things that happened to our family. Their birthdays were in July. Hers was July 3rd and his was July 5th, so the 4th of July was one of the biggest summer holidays we celebrated in our family because we celebrated their birthdays on that day. The entire family celebrated with a cake, a barbeque with crabs, and, of course, drinks and dancing. We had the best summers at my grandparents' home. Their home was the middle ground where everyone could come.

    At my grandmother's funeral, we were leaving the burial site to head back to the cars for the repast. My mom and my cousin were arm and arm with one another when they fell in a hole that was not completely covered after burying another person. Unfortunately, that didn't make matters any better for my mom. She started feeling pain in her back and legs (and is now disabled). She had her hip replaced many years later. She told me then that she understood what the pain felt like. I know all too well about hip pain. I have bursitis and arthritis as a result of my skating accident. I experience the most pain in my hips when it rains. I even experience pain when it's super cold outside.

Pushing Through

"Be yourself; everyone else is already taken." – Oscar Wilde

Charise Marie
Chapter Two:
Baby Brown's Arrival

1997

We met and had an instant "love" connection, or so we thought. Maybe it was "puppy love." We became boyfriend and girlfriend not long after meeting each other. We were both eighteen years young. We had a good relationship. We spent time together, mostly at his grandmother's house where he lived.

He had one daughter whom he adored and took care of. I knew that one day I wanted to be a mother, but I wanted to be a wife first. About halfway into our relationship, we decided we wanted to have a child together, and I became pregnant instead. I found out I was pregnant just four days before I graduated from a trade school; I was to receive my diploma in Medical Office Management. This was a technical trade school I went to after I graduated high school in 1996. I was a little skeptical about the relationship because early on in our relationship he had told me about his religion and our religions were totally different.

I was born and raised Catholic and he was now Muslim, I don't know when he converted. He asked whether I wanted to get married, but "take my *Shahada*" was what he said. That is the Islamic term for converting to the Islamic reli-

Pushing Through

gion.

I didn't know what he was speaking of at the time, so I said no. I didn't really think that changing my religion was what I wanted to do. I also didn't think about what I wanted my child's religion to be either, other than the religion with which I was already familiar. I guess that was something for me to consider. I then told my boyfriend that I would prefer for our child to decide on their own what religion they wanted to be once they were older.

My first few visits to the doctor's office for prenatal care were good, except for the fact that I was known as high risk due to my severe asthma. I also was diagnosed with having migraines. The fact that I was on so many medications was also a factor in being labeled high risk. My visits weren't bad in the beginning. I went in every few weeks. On the day of the ultrasound to find out the gender of my baby, its legs were closed. I had to wait until my next visit to find out the sex.

On my next visit, I had my fingers crossed that baby Brown had its legs wide open for mommy and doctor to see, and lo and behold, yup, they were open. We could clearly see exactly what gender baby Brown was. I had been hoping for a girl, but they told me I was having a boy. Now I had to think of names for my son. My son. It felt weird saying "my son" when I was so used to saying I was having a girl. I was used to saying "my daughter," but now I had to get used to saying I was having a boy.

I was a little disappointed that I was having a boy, to be honest. I asked numerous friends whether I would still

Charise Marie

love him as much as if he were a girl. They all told me that I would still love him the same. They also let me know that it was natural to feel that way, but it would pass in due time and my feelings for him would be big and warm hearted.

My doctor had me to take things easy because of being high risk. Plus, I had to be careful of every medication I took. Some medications are not safe to take during pregnancies.

My son's father and I didn't last through my pregnancy. We broke up around six months into it. He called me almost every day to see what I was up to and how the baby and I were doing. He would tell me not to eat pork because it wasn't healthy for our child. He also said, "No child of his should be having pork unwillingly shoved down his throat." He didn't eat pork. I ignored him most times as I was raised on eating pork. My family didn't tell us what we could and couldn't eat.

Around this time, I was getting bigger and bigger. My doctor watched me closely; I went in almost once a week now. It was time for me to think of names. I asked the kids in my neighborhood to think of some boy names to help me name my son. I wanted it to start with a "J." His dad's name started with a "J" (but I knew he would not be named after him), and my mother's name started with one too. My nephew told me that he had twins in his class and told me their names. I said one of the names sounded perfect. I would name my son after that one little boy.

My son was due the day before his dad's birthday; that's how we planned our baby. We had planned for him to be due

Pushing Through

sometime in September near his dad's birthday. I was due to have him on September 20th, but for some odd reason, he didn't want to come out.

I did have a nasty fall at his dad's house in the kitchen of his apartment. I went to visit him, and as I was leaving, I missed the step in the kitchen and fell right on my bottom. I was scared something happened to my baby. I called the hospital and was told that if I didn't feel any movements or if I saw any blood when I went to the bathroom to come into the hospital and be checked. Luckily, I felt him kicking and moving and there was no blood.

My doctor scheduled me for an induced labor on Sunday, October 4th, 1998, at 7:30 p.m. because my son had yet to introduce himself to the world. He was two weeks overdue. I went to the hospital with my mom and a female relative, who stayed with me the entire time. My dad popped in the night I was induced, but left to flirt with one of the nurses. The nurse placed the inducing gel inside of me at 7:30 p.m. and said that I was only one centimeter dilated.

I jumped up around midnight and ran to the bathroom, thinking I had to pee. Nothing came out. I stood over the toilet and pushed and pushed, but still nothing came out. I called the nurse and told her how I felt. She let me know that I was only two centimeters dilated and that I had a long way to go. My mom and my female relative just laughed and said, "Lie down, girl."

The nurse came in with the doctor around 8:00 the next morning, October 5th, to check on me. They told me that I was only five centimeters. The doctor asked whether I was

Charise Marie

in pain and I said that I wasn't; I was just very uncomfortable.

The doctor then asked whether I wanted an epidural and explained what it was. I agreed. He left and my nurse went to get another nurse to help her give me the epidural. They told me to sit up with my legs dangling over the side of the hospital bed. One held me tight in a ball so I wouldn't move, and the other nurse gave me the epidural in my lower back.

After the shot they said that they were going to poke me with something to break my water. I was so high that I couldn't remember most of what was going on. Around the time I was given the epidural, my ex-boyfriend, the baby's father, called to see if I had given birth to our son. I was half out of it and didn't know what he, or I, were saying. I remember my mom screaming next to me. She said to get off the phone with him because he should be at the hospital with me. I got frustrated with him because he wasn't there and hung up.

By the time the afternoon rolled around, I was irritated. I started to get anxious as well. When was he going to come out? I'd been there for hours.

Later that evening around 8:00, they came in to check me again.

I said, "Look, it's been more than twenty-four hours since I got here; get him out of me."

The doctor came in, checked me, and told me that I was at eight centimeters. They returned forty-five minutes or

Pushing Through

so later because I was getting on their nerves. They checked again and said I was close. I was nine centimeters now. They told me that I would be delivering him very soon. I said, "No, now! Now!" The nurse said, "I'll be back."

The nurse came back and checked me and said I gone back to eight centimeters so she called the doctor. He came in and said, "We are going to have to rush you in for an emergency C-section."

I said, "Well hurry up and get him out of me."

I was very concerned because I had heard horror stories of babies being left in the womb with no amniotic fluid. My mom was in the room with me. I told her to make sure to take pictures of him coming out; just keep clicking the camera. She laughed and said, "Why, girl?"

I said, "I just saw that movie where they switched the babies at birth, and I will be damned if someone switches my baby. Take five hundred pictures of him!" She took pictures but laughed at me.

I felt a tug, and as they pulled him out of me, I think he got stuck because I did fall when I was five or six months pregnant. But soon, out came my big, beautiful, baby boy, who was born on October 5th, 1998, weighing ten pounds, two ounces.

Yes, you read it right; he was a big, bright baby with a head full of hair. They put him on my chest for a second and then rushed him to the Neonatal Intensive Care Unit (NICU) because he was breathing too fast and had fluid in his lungs.

Charise Marie

They let me touch him through the incubator. I laid there and cried as they numbed my belly to stitch me up. I wanted to be with my baby. After they stitched me up, they gave me pain medicine and took me to my room.

I jumped up in pain around 6:00 the next morning and demanded to see my baby. I questioned, "How do you not let a mother see her baby?"

The nurse finally came in after making me go to the bathroom and having something to eat. I was very upset because I had not seen my son since I had had him the night before. I was knocked out from the medications given to me after they stitched up my belly.

She took me down to the NICU and had me stand up slowly over the incubators because I was still in a lot of pain. She said, "I'll have you stand this way because you might see the names in the front. Which one is your baby?"

I said, "That one," and pointed to my son.

"You're correct. That's baby Brown."

"Yes, that's baby Brown and I'm in love already."

"How did you know which one he was?" she asked.

"He looks just like my grandfather, my Pop Pop."

She laughed and wheeled me over to the second incubator as I cried. He was hooked up to a few monitors, but nothing as bad as some of the other babies in there. The

Pushing Through

nurse took me to the side, near a table and television, away from the other babies.

She said, "Why are you crying?"

"Why is he in here; I want him well, but why?" I cried.

She said, "Baby, he is the healthiest baby in here, trust me."

"Well, why is he in here?" I asked.

"We had to monitor his breathing and he had fluid in his lungs." She continued, "It's okay, he will be just fine. Now some of the other babies are really sad stories." It didn't ease my pain a whole lot, but some.

The hospital released me the third day after my delivery but kept my son. I was livid, but I wanted him well. My mom called a local children's hospital closer to where we lived to ask if we could place him in their NICU. He was transported there the next day. I then traveled back and forth from home to the hospital every day.

I ended up having severe pains where my C-section incision was as it wasn't healing correctly due to all my traveling. I was overextending myself. I spoke with a nurse at the children's hospital and asked whether I could stay somewhere in the hospital to be close to my son. I truly hated having to be away from him because he was just born. She contacted hospital officials and found out that I could stay in a room with some other parents. I didn't care that I was sleeping on a cot; I just wanted to be closer to my

Charise Marie

baby. He was in the NICU for a total of seven days. He was released on Monday, October 12th, three days after being admitted to the children's hospital.

I was extremely happy that he was much better and being released. I still had to find a way to take care of myself, though, since one of my staples had popped out from all the running around and making sure my son was okay. The nurses gave me plenty of gauze and cleaning solution.

On my son's first day home, most of my family was at the house waiting for him. My grandfather called me and gave me advice that has stuck with me since that day.

He said, "Mook," which is the nickname he gave me at birth, "don't you let everyone kiss all over him. His baby skin may break out and you don't know where people's mouths have been. You hear me?"

"Yes, okay Pop Pop."

He continued with, "And definitely don't let them walk in off the street holding him either; better yet, you make everybody wash their nasty ass hands before touching him. You hear me, Mook?"

"Yes, Pop Pop."

He said, "Are you listening to me?"

"Yes, Pop Pop."

Pushing Through

I made sure from that day forward that anyone looking to touch my baby had to wash their hands first. Pop Pop was right. People come in after touching money, filthy things out in the street, door knobs, cars, and some people don't wash their hands correctly after using bathrooms either. I wish people would realize that when you touch a baby's hand, they put their hands in their mouth and that's nothing but germs. People come in off the street and rub their cheeks and wonder why babies' faces break out sometimes.

I was so happy he was home I barely had time take care of me. My C-section incision took a long time to heal. I had my son's first appointment at the children's hospital where I signed him up as a patient three weeks after he was born. My brother had to go with me because my son was more than ten pounds when he was born, so we knew he had gained a few more ounces since being out of the hospital. He was too heavy for me to carry after my C-section. My brother carried him in the car seat that was given to me at my baby shower. I carried his baby bag with his diapers, toys, and bottles.

We were standing in a packed elevator when a woman looked down and said, "Oh, such a beautiful baby girl."

I said, "It's a boy."

Another lady said, "Oh, he is adorable. How old is he? He looks like he is around three months old."

"He is only three weeks old," I said.

"What!"

Charise Marie

"He was a big baby when he was born. He was ten pounds, two ounces," I explained.

She said, "Sheesh, he was a big baby. Well, congratulations."

"Thank you."

His appointment went well that day. I got home and told my mom about it. I told her how we were in the elevator and I got upset that some women thought he was a girl. My mom laughed and said it was cute when people mistake a boy for a girl because that just means he was pretty.

Now, in my opinion, you don't want someone to mistake a girl for a boy; that's not pretty. My mom laughed. I laughed too, and told her that was good because my baby was the most handsome baby boy I had ever seen.

A few short weeks later, my ex-boyfriend called me pretending that he was concerned about our son. He later told me that he didn't think he was his son. This belief is the reason he broke up with me and why he hadn't come to the hospital. Even when our son was in the NICU for a week, he didn't call and didn't show.

I was like, "This is a joke, right?"

He said, "No, I believe you were sleeping with other men."

Pushing Through

I laughed because he knew I was only with him, but I was baffled as to why he was accusing me. I quickly found out that this claim was one-way men tried to get out of raising their children. I shrugged him off and told him that I would be raising our son on my own with help from my family. I made sure that he knew that I didn't need him and neither did my son. I felt that it was important for my son to have his father, but if he didn't want to be his father, why would I push him to be? Although my son would need a father figure around, I felt that my brother, stepdad, and a host of other men around would do just fine.

January 1999

My sperm donor, my son's father that is, said that he wanted me to pay for a paternity test since he didn't believe our son was his. I refused to pay because I knew he was the father. He claimed that the only way he would take care of our son was if he knew he really was his. I laughed and said it would be a cold day in hell before I paid for that test. Ironically, soon after that conversation I saw a television commercial on a paternity test flash across the screen and I had a bright idea. I called *The Ricki Lake Show*, *The Jenny Jones Show*, and *The Montel Williams Show*, but none of them returned my call. I also called *The Forgive or Forget Show* with Mother Love, and the producers called me back almost immediately. They booked the trip for me, my son, his dad, his cousin, and my high school friend Shelly to be on the show. We went on the television show and stayed in the New York hotel they put us in. The producers kept asking me questions backstage about our relationship, and I answered them. They kept asking this one question that was pissing me off: "If he doesn't come through the curtains,

Charise Marie

what are you going to do?"

I looked clearly at the lady and said, "He's coming through those curtains."

She said, "But no, I need an answer on if he doesn't."

"I don't want to have to tell you again, he's coming through that door. But let me play your game with you. If he does not come through that door, which he will, that will mean he is not my son's father, which he is, I will go behind that stage and find his ass and pull him on stage. Are you good with that answer?"

"Okay!" she said.

"This is not a joke; this is my life that he seems to think is a joke. I don't think this is funny. Since he didn't want to help me pay for a paternity test, we are here getting a free one. My son is his so I don't want to hear anything else since I'm already nervous enough."

Once we got on stage, my ex tried to say that I had been sleeping with all his friends, which he knew wasn't true. I don't know if he wanted to make himself look good, make me look bad, or even if they told him backstage to make me look bad. Then it was the moment of truth after answering all the questions that Mother Love asked. They told me to walk over to the door and the black curtain. I stood there, and although nervous about being on national television, I wasn't nervous about him coming through that door. They opened the door and he was there, just like I said.

Pushing Through

Mother Love told him to pick his face up off the floor. "You did all this on television to this girl, and you're this little boy's father." I started crying. Mother Love asked why I was crying and I told her that I wasn't unfaithful to him and I wasn't promiscuous. For him to make me out as a whore on television had me furious. She said, "Let me read the results. You are 99.98% that precious baby boy's father." They brought our son out on stage for his television debut, and everyone melted like I did while holding him.

I got home from the show and my family was furious at my son's dad. I was told my grandfather had a hit out on him because of the things he had said about me, but I told my mom to please tell Pop Pop not to make matters worse; to let God handle him. They say you reap what you sow, and he seemed to be sowing the wrong seeds.

A few months later, he called me and acted like he wanted to be a father to our son. He asked me to bring him over his house. My girlfriend Tanya told me that she would ride with me. My son was now about eight months old and his father hadn't seen him since we had been on the show when he was three months old.

We got into an argument as we sat outside in his enclosed porch, and he took my son into his house and locked the door. I threatened to call the cops, and he came outside and punched me in the back of my head. I blacked out. My girlfriend jumped up and tried to reach him, but he ran back in the house and locked the door like a coward. He then came outside and threw our son into my arms. I called the cops and left to go home. I later got a restraining order against him and he tried to deny everything.

Charise Marie

See, this wasn't the first time he had put his hands on me. During our relationship, a few times, he roughed me up, slapped me, and even burned me with matches or lighters. I eventually realized that this behavior was not love, it was abuse, and I left him completely alone.

Even after all these years, he has never taken care of our son. As for child support, he was court ordered to pay seventy-five dollars a week, but I only ever received two or three payments. He couldn't be found in the system after about five years, so the child services courts sent me a letter explaining that my son would no longer receive child support because there was no activity on the case. My son, who is a teenager now, has run into him once or twice on the street, but that is it. There have been no phone calls, no birthday cards, and certainly no payments. Just nothing. He has always been able to get in touch with us because my parents have never moved. He ran into my mom and son one day as they were going into the house. He spoke with our son, but that was as far as it went.

Pushing Through

"No one is going to love you if you don't love yourself." – Unknown

Charise Marie
Chapter Three:
Weight No More

    I suffered from being overweight and having Polycystic Ovarian Syndrome (PCOS) for years. My primary care doctor explained that my hormones were abnormal and this was the reason my menstrual cycle was irregular. PCOS was also associated with obesity, high blood pressure, and diabetes. I let him know that my cycle came every few months. "What does this mean?" I asked him. "Will I develop diabetes? Will I develop high blood pressure and be on medication the rest of my life? Will I be unable to have more children? What does all of this mean?"

    He said, "You must lose a lot of weight. You're in the 250-pound range. Maybe you should seek out a bariatric doctor for weight-loss surgery."

    "No, no, no, no, no, I will not be having any of those dangerous surgeries," I stated clearly.

    He said, "You're on the verge of being diabetic and your blood pressure is high; I'm putting you on medication."

    I left his office thinking I would not be on high blood pressure medicine the rest of my life. I gained seventy pounds when I was pregnant with my son. I lost most of it easily, but because my asthma is so severe, I'm always on

Pushing Through

steroids. I quickly gained most of it back.

Around this time I began thinking that I wanted to start dating again. Dominic and I met when we were around fourteen years old, but over the years, after high school, we lost contact. When he came into my life, we had a pretty good relationship, except for the fact that I told him I wanted to explore being with women. Dominic told me no, that's not a good idea. He asked me to marry him and I said yes. I thought that if I had a happy life with him, I would forget all about being with women. He never said anything about my weight or weight gain. He just told me he loved me for me. He was very good with my son as well. He played with him, taught him things, and treated him like he was his own son. We talked about having children. After months of being in our relationship, we stopped using protection some of the time because we wanted kids soon. We set a wedding date and our families were very excited for us. I couldn't understand for the life of me why I never became pregnant while we were together. I concluded that it wasn't me, it had to be him. I had a kid and he had none.

2002–2004

In 2002 our relationship started going downhill. My feelings for women were always there, but they were becoming stronger. I started having feelings for girls when I was sixteen years old, but I always suppressed them, because let's face it, growing up gay is not the norm. I started seeking out women on phone chat lines while Dominic was at school or work. I never slept with a woman until later on

Charise Marie

because I was way too nervous to try.

My relationship with my fiancé Dominic of a year and a half soon ended. Our break up was bound to come sooner or later. He started to see that I wasn't into him as much anymore, so he began cheating. I didn't care because I had started talking to a woman not long after we broke up. I know I gained at least thirty pounds or more during my relationship with him. After the relationship ended, I tried to focus more on raising my son, working out, and buying a house.

I ran into his mom a few years later and she told me that Dominic had a little boy and girl. I questioned myself what it could have been if he had two children now with someone else, but never had any with me because I still had the one son. It had me thinking that maybe there could've an issue with me, but what

I saw him years later at a department store and he mentioned that his mom saw me. He was with his sister and his nephew and they saw how big my son was. They spoke to each other, but my son was very young when he and I were together so he didn't remember him.

My phone kept ringing off the hook the entire morning around 8 a.m. I finally heard my cousin's voice on the answering machine telling me to pick up the phone because Pop Pop had passed away. I jumped up and was like, "What did she just say?" I called my cousin back and she said, "Someone is on their way to pick you up and bring you to our grandparents' house." I asked her what happened and she told me that our grandfather, our Pop Pop, our patri-

Pushing Through

arch, had passed away. I was devastated with the thought of another death.

Why God, why?

I called my ex-fiancé Dominic as he and I were still working on our relationship, and he came right to my side. He told me that he knew all too well about losing a grandfather as he had lost his the year before. He told me everything was going to be alright and that my Pop Pop was in a better place. Of course, I knew that, but I just didn't want to hear it. I wanted my Pop Pop and my Nana back here with me.

After the death of my grandfather, I tried to eat healthier, as I've tried before in the past, but it just didn't work for me. I tried everything I could to lose weight. I tried all kinds of new recipes, different lifestyles, just about anything to get the weight off me.

I moved into my grandparents' home where I was raised. I stayed in that home until I purchased my own house the day before Thanksgiving in 2003. As a single mother with a five-year-old son, I had it pretty hard when it came to saving money and buying a house. I lost my job in February of 2004 and had gallbladder surgery at the end of that month. After losing my job of two years, I sat around and ate, ate, ate. As a result, I packed on more pounds. I wasn't depressed; I just had low moments in my life that may have shifted my focus a few times.

Charise Marie

2004–2009

I visited my primary care doctor in 2004 and he told me my weight and high blood pressure had come down some although it wasn't enough weight loss because it had been only seven or eight pounds. He didn't take me off my medications, but I decided to stop my pressure medication. The only medicine I would continue taking, I decided, would be my asthma medication. I felt as though I was fine now. He did add a new medication for my migraines since the other one was not working. Once I received the new migraine medication at home I read the description and side effects. I quickly learned that this medication was an antidepressant and can alter your mood. It affects chemicals in the brain that may be unbalanced in people with depression. I was ready to take it back but once I saw I was on a low dose for migraines but saw it was given at a higher dose for depression I thought nothing or it. I did however notice it said rapid weight gain was one of the side effects as well.

I started a new relationship in May of 2004, this time with a woman. It was my first lesbian relationship. Most people seem to think that once a woman leaves a relationship with a man and begins one with a woman, she is either confused or has been hurt by men. That wasn't my case. I had quite a few male friends interested in me; I just wasn't feeling it. I had no desire to be sexual with men anymore. My ex-boyfriend even asked me after we broke up whether I had started messing around with women while we were together, and I was honest with him and told him yes. I started seeing women right at our break up point.

Pushing Through

Once again, I began seeking out women on phone chat lines and that's was how I met Chrissy. Being in a new relationship always feels great. You're getting to know one another, having fun, going new places and, of course, trying out restaurants. With all the happiness I was experiencing, I was starting to balloon. I was getting bigger and bigger.

In 2007 I decided to start a business. I was going to be a romance consultant with a known adult-toy company. This job gave me a chance to learn how to run a business and come out of my comfort zone; I was shy around people who were not family or close friends. I'm not sure if the shyness was a result of just being me or being pleasantly plump.

Later that year, I had a pretty bad asthma attack and was rushed to the hospital. I saw my primary care doctor shortly after and he changed my asthma medicine. I told him that the hospital put me on steroids again. He said to be careful because steroids tend to cause weight gain. I told him I knew that because I had been taking steroids for years, which was one of the reasons why I had so much weight on me. My weight skyrocketed in 1998 after the birth of my son. I was around two hundred pounds when I first became pregnant and I gained seventy pounds during the pregnancy. I was able to lose nearly half of it after giving birth, but then was in the hospital for a pretty bad asthma attack, so they put me on steroids again as was the regular routine. I was now looking at 335 pounds. That was the biggest I had ever been in my life.

I knew taking the steroids would be something that would make me gain weight but now knowing the migraine medicine did the same. I was instructed to only take the

Charise Marie

migraine medicine at night. It was so hard to take it when a migraine would hit during the day. I nearly had to sleep that medicine off for 6-8 hours and could not be awaken. Chrissy knew when to stay away from me because that medication would make me a monster. I would wake up snapping if she awakens me any time before the 6-8 hours was up. I would literally turn into someone she didn't know. I hated taking it but it worked so good for my migraines.

Chrissy and I decided to "get married." We had a very nice civil union/wedding ceremony and reception in 2008. Gay marriage wasn't legal in my state at the time, so we just did a ceremony and reception without the paperwork. Not long after we had our ceremony, we received our pictures back and that was when I realized how heavy I looked. They say pictures are worth a thousand words. My wedding pictures were worth a thousand tears. I was upset, not at the pictures per se, but how I looked in them. Of course, my family and friends all said I looked beautiful, but truth be told, they might have just been being nice because they loved me. She even cried as I came down the aisle and once I arrived she said mamas, her nickname for me, you look beautiful.

I looked at the pictures and was kind of disgusted at how big I was. I remember on that day how I felt so beautiful and kept asking my bridesmaids whether I looked okay. They all replied that I looked great. "This is your day, enjoy it," they said. I looked at my best friend Heaven and said, "You always tell me the truth; how do I look?" She has always been in my corner and has told me that no matter how heavy I am that I am always beautiful. I looked at her that day and she said, "Baby, you're always beautiful to me. Now stop

Pushing Through

worrying and let's go celebrate your love."

I contacted my doctor the end of 2008 and he brought up bariatric surgery again because of me gaining more weight. This time, however, I was really considering it. In 2009 I started doing research on bariatric surgeries, also known as weight-loss surgery, or WLS. I came across gastric bypass and the LAP-BAND surgeries. I sought out a bariatric doctor in my area. Chrissy and I attended a new-patient session of questions and answers with all the information on surgeries. After doing a little more research on him and which weight-loss surgery would be best for me, I decided on the LAP-BAND. I had another visit with my primary care doctor and I filled him in on my visit with the bariatric surgery doctor. He told me that having surgery may be a great idea. He said, "I think you should go for the gastric bypass."

"I have chosen to get the LAP-BAND," I explained.

He said, "Okay, that seems a little dangerous."

"They all do," I said. "I just have to leave it in God's hands. He is the only one who can wake me up from that surgery table."

I started having regular appointments with the bariatric doctor. He let me know that my highest recorded weight was 344 pounds, and with my head down, I agreed. Being ashamed of myself was an understatement; I was very embarrassed by that high number. He reminded me that my starting weight with him was 324 pounds.

Charise Marie

    I followed the advice that the bariatric doctor and the nutritionist gave. I lost fifteen pounds before surgery. I filled in my family and friends on my weight-loss process; they were very scared for me. As soon as I mentioned I was going to have weight-loss surgery, they were all completely against it. Of course, everyone has read the horror stories of people dying from having complications during some of these surgeries. My family and friends asked me why was I considering surgery, and, with a sad face, I provided multiple reasons why I felt having surgery would be best for me: I was tired of being big; it was not attractive being huge; I didn't feel comfortable anymore in my clothing; I was on the verge of being diabetic, and most of the people in my family, from my grandparents to my mother, aunts, uncles, and cousins all have diabetes; I have high blood pressure.

    In addition, because of the surgery I had on my hips when I was nine years old, the pain I have from all the weight causes a lot of additional pain too. I wake up in pain because I have arthritis and bursitis, but having this extra weight on my five-foot, four-inch body frame is too much. I also want to be able to have more children in the future. Being this big is causing me not to have a menstrual cycle, which means I can't have children. I'm still young and have only one child. Don't you think I want to have more children? Plus, I hate walking into stores and not being able to fit into what they have, even in the big-girl section. Sizes in most stores are not really plus-size; they are much smaller in certain stores. It is embarrassing walking into a store and not finding the size that I need, even in a plus-size store. I'm a size twenty-four now, and my biggest size was twenty-eight.

Pushing Through

My family and friends continued to tell me how beautiful I already was, but I didn't want to hear that now. It was a little too late for that. Some days, I've felt low. I've never had high self-esteem or low self-esteem. I've always said I've had low moments, but never low self-esteem. I wasn't suffering from low self-esteem at the time either.

I ended my relationship with Chrissy in September 2009. It was devastating, but it was time for us to go our separate ways. The stress of the relationship had me working out at home, but I started to become a little depressed. We tried a few times to make our relationship last, but it just wasn't working for us. Luckily, we were not legally married. Thanksgiving came around and we spoke over the phone, but we were sad because it was our first holiday without one another so we spent Christmas together. She and my son adored each other so it was nice to spend the holiday together as a family one last time. I expressed to her that sitting around together these last few years had not been healthy for us. I had gained a lot of weight, and that both of us being comfortable with it was not good. She gained weight during our relationship as well, but not as much as I did. I told her that I had started preparing to have weight-loss surgery, and she said she wanted to be there, along with my best friend Heaven, when I had the surgery. I told her I appreciated her support and was glad she was able to be by my side when the day came.

Charise Marie

"If you change the way you look at things, the things you look at change." – Wayne Dyer

Pushing Through

Chapter Four:

First Day of My New Life

February 2010

I opened my eyes while lying in the bed and said my prayers.

God, I thank you for waking me up this morning. I ask that you watch over me, my family, and my friends. The day is finally here, and God, I'm extremely excited, nervous, and scared. I ask that you wake me up from that operating table in great condition with the foreign object inside of me. I pray in Jesus' name, amen.

My ex Chrissy and my best friend Heaven went to the hospital with me. I weighed in at 307 pounds the morning of my LAP-BAND surgery. The nurse who tried to draw my blood had a difficult time because I was not supposed to have any food or drinks after 7:00 the night before my surgery. As a result, my body was so dehydrated that drawing blood was a very hard and long process. Ouch! She literally got two drops of blood, finally.

I went into surgery and came out. I opened my eyes and said, "Thank you, God." I screamed for a nurse. "I want to talk to my son! Get me a phone; I need to hear my son's voice. Please get me a phone now, please!" I talked to my

Charise Marie

son and my mom. I told them that I was out of surgery and was only in minimal pain.

My ex Chrissy and best friend Heaven came upstairs with stuffed animals for me. We were happy to see one another. They asked about my pain and questioned whether I was supposed to be up and walking. I said that the doctor suggested that I move about so no clots would form in my body.

My bariatric doctor came in later and said everything went well; he would be discharging me within an hour. The first few days I was to be on clear liquids such as broths, water, tea with no sugar, and Jell–O. I didn't feel much pain, just a little discomfort—gassy discomfort to be exact.

I was tired of drinking water; I never really liked water to begin with. Per the doctor and nutritionist's list of what a bariatric patient should be eating per week, I was now on full liquids: unsweetened juices, decaffeinated tea, strained creamy soups, etc. By week three I was able to have pureed or soft foods such as a scrambled egg, cheese, Greek yogurt with chunks of fruit in it, and soft fruits.

After those first few weeks I was able to eat tuna salad, chicken salad, lots of meats with protein (but the softer versions), so most had to have some kind of broth in them to soften them up. I was also told that the days of drinking and eating at the same time were now over. I could no longer drink and eat my food at the same time because drinking liquids made me full quicker. I felt that after the surgery I had started to become more emotional, something that I wasn't before. I would cry over all kinds of things now and

Pushing Through

most never made any sense.

I started a new relationship a few months later. We started dating, and I had to instantly express that I had undergone LAP-BAND surgery so there was no way I would be able to eat as much as I used to. Going on dates didn't seem fun anymore. I was getting angry that I couldn't eat everything I had ordered. But that was the point—not to eat everything on my plate! That's where the extra weight had come from: eating everything. Movies, dancing, and dinner sounded great, but when you're used to eating your entire meal, these things were no longer any fun for me. Plus, I had to eat healthier choices. Healthier choices always seem to cost so much more money.

I hid my surgery from my friends on social media for a long time because of the negative comments I had heard from people in my family, the community, friends, and even people I didn't know. Therefore, not many people knew of my LAP-BAND surgery. Plus, my weight wasn't coming off like I thought it would with the LAP-BAND like it did for others I saw at the doctors' offices, on the internet, and on television.

One thing about me is that I have no patience. I'm impulsive too. It's definitely not a good combination, I know. I worked out (but not as much as I should have), and I ate healthy. I followed exactly what the doctor said. I saw the doctor and not much weight had come off. He asked what I was doing, and I told him that I had followed what he suggested. So why wasn't the weight coming off? What was it that I was doing that I should not be doing? What was it that I was not doing that I should be doing? Why me? Why get this surgery and have it not work for me? Why was my food starting to get stuck at the top of my stomach above the LAP-BAND? He loosened up my LAP-BAND a little bit and said to continue what I was doing. He told me to take my time and the weight would start to fall off. It had only been a few months.

I saw my doctor a few weeks later and still had only lost one or two pounds. I explained to him that my food was getting stuck even more, so he loosened my LAP-BAND again. A few months later I had gained some weight, so he tightened it up just a little. This cycle went on for the next few months.

My new mate, Kimmy, I call her Tiny for a nickname, saw me struggle with the LAP-BAND a lot over that first year. I would eat eggs for breakfast and they would get stuck, so I would try to wash them down with a little water or a drink. By then I was learning how to cheat, so to speak. I sipped water most of the time when I ate now. The weight was slowly coming off. It went up and down for quite some time. I was working out at home. I was doing more walking and working out on my gaming console, which had fitness DVDs that I would move and dance to. I was scared to go to a gym, which is why I never signed up. I was afraid of the looks and the comments I might get when I was on machines. Besides that, I had never been in a gym so I wouldn't know what to get on or use. I didn't want to look foolish on a machine by not knowing how to use it.

Pushing Through

March 2011

By 2011 I had become friends with a lot of people in the weight-loss community. I had a separate social media page just for weight-loss friends. I started watching a lot of their blogging videos. Many people in the weight-loss community, or the WLS community as it's affectionately called, did weight-loss videos. They showed the food they ate, how they worked out, and how the weight-loss surgery worked for them. I watched the many men and women who made videos on their weight-loss journey for months. I watched videos from people who had the LAP-BAND, gastric bypass, duodenal switch, and the gastric sleeve. I had never heard of the duodenal switch or the gastric sleeve. When I went in for my surgery consultations, I was only told of the gastric bypass and the LAP-BAND surgeries. I became very curious as to what these other two surgeries were. I saw how these men and women lost weight, gained weight, and lost friends and family members due to jealousy. Some had even lost spouses, girlfriends, or boyfriends. I was scared. I thought, *Will my fiancée Tiny leave me? Once I lose a lot of weight, will I be looked at differently or will I be loved any less? Will my outer appearance affect our relationship? Will my outer appearance change my outlook on life? What if my fiancée leaves me? Will I become depressed? Will I start eating unhealthy foods and gain my weight back?*

Wow! I never thought these questions would be things to think about. I questioned my Tiny's love for me, and she looked at me with a weird facial expression. I asked her, "Do you love me?"

She said, "Yes, I love you. Why would you ask me that?"

Charise Marie

I said, "I just wanted to know, that's all."

July 2011

    I finally signed up for my first gym membership. I had been doing a little dancing at home since my surgery. I moved about with some exercise and dancing games, or I played tennis or bowling on the gaming console to keep myself active. But that didn't seem to be working like I wanted. After joining the gym, I would leave work at 4:00 p.m. to get to the gym by 5:00. I was scared to go to the gym, but I was very determined to get the weight off me. I just knew by going into this gym, people would see this big girl, me, and try to think of a reason why I would be there. I quickly thought about how this gym was the place I really needed to be. I had to stop telling myself all the negative stuff that would kill my chances of getting on with my life. If I told myself I needed to be in this gym to get the weight off, that's what I needed to tell myself. I started off very slowly with some weights and the bikes. I went to the gym three to four times a week and on weekends also. I rode the bike for twenty to twenty-five minutes. I then went in the weight room and worked out on the different weight-lifting machines.

    As I was leaving one day, the receptionist asked me whether I had signed up for a trainer. I told her no because I didn't have money for that. She let me know that the first session was free, and then I could determine if I wanted to continue to use them. I said sure, and signed up with a trainer. She scheduled my appointment for the following week, which was the soonest he was available. I was scared to death. What would this man think of me when he saw

Pushing Through

me? I continued going in the rest of the week, convincing myself that during our appointment he could at least point me in the right direction as to which machines to use, how to use them, and what exercises to do.

I went in the next week and met the trainer. He showed me how to use the different weight machines, the other bikes, the elliptical machine, and even the treadmill. Now I looked at him like he was crazy. I said, "I mean no harm, but I am deathly afraid of falling on those elliptical and treadmill machines. You will not see my fat ass flying across the room."

We both laughed, and he said, "You can take your time with each one; go at your own pace." I was still trying not to hear it. He helped me get on the elliptical and I didn't like it one bit. Plus, my legs on that machine would have me in the hospital because of the pain. I tried the treadmill, and to my surprise, I liked it. I did exactly what he said and took my time. I was on the treadmill for about twenty minutes while he continued to show me the speeds and incline levels. I said, "I don't know about any of that," and he said, "That is pretty much it. If you want me to become your trainer or want any other one of the trainers, please let me know." I said okay, and thanked him for his time.

After he showed me how to use the machines, I was ready to keep moving. I went in there every other day after work and usually one day on the weekends. I'd put my headphones on with my music and just go. I still thought that everyone was looking at me, but I remembered a few people telling me that the more you think negative thoughts, the more you will keep negative feelings toward doing what you want and need to do. In order to get positive results, you need to change your mind to positive thoughts. I told them that they were correct because if I kept thinking people were looking at me, I wasn't going to want to come back. We were all in there for one reason or another and that was to lose weight or focus on some part of our body image. Why should I be ashamed to come in here and try to get my health together?

I went in one Saturday morning, had music blasting in my ear, and was walking on the treadmill. I was in a groove; I was ready to go. By now I had gotten up to about forty-five minutes on the treadmill each time I went in. Then this guy on my left looked at my treadmill. I caught him looking, but neither he nor I said anything at first. He then said, "Excuse me, can I tell you something?"

I looked at him like, "What do you have to tell me, sir?" but I said, "Sure."

He said, "If you put your speed up just a little bit and then your incline some, you will lose a little bit more quickly. It's just a suggestion. I had to learn that myself as I didn't know."

I said, "Thank you for the information, but I have leg problems and I try not to go too fast or even run on these things."

I did put the incline up just a bit and the speed up a little too. He went on doing his workout, and although I hadn't asked him for his help, it did help me out a little bit later.

Pushing Through

August 2011

Sometime during the summer, I decided to leave the adult-toy companies that I was with and start my own. I had already done some research on starting my own adult-toy company and I did. That is when *Party with Mook* was born. It was a slight challenge in the beginning as I had to create my own website and set my own prices, as well as run the parties. It became easier after the first few months. I had needed to challenge myself to see how easy it could be to start my own business.

I heard about a weight-loss convention some people had in the East Coast area in August 2010. We, Tiny and I, attended my first (their second) weight-loss convention in Atlantic City. It was pretty nice being in a little tavern. Everyone seemed to love my T-shirt. It had a picture of the "big" me on the back and said "she is behind me now." I was happy that I had lost a nice amount of weight, but I still had some ways to go.

We nibbled on the food, took pictures, and had some drinks. It was a nice time. Meeting people I had watched make videos in the weight-loss community was fun. Everyone seemed friendly. The people who sat at our table were nice, and we all talked about the different surgeries we had undergone. We also discussed the ups and downs with having the different surgeries. Some expressed how they got sick if they ate or drank particular kinds of foods, and some could no longer eat that kind of food. I was like, Wow! I just thought about the times some of my food would get stuck. Even eggs got stuck, softly scrambled eggs. We exchanged social media page names, said our goodbyes, and went our separate ways. We continue to follow each other daily on social media.

October 2011

Searching online and watching my friends make videos became the only thing I liked to watch. I came across a few women who spoke about having revision surgery from LAP-BAND to gastric bypass and LAP-BAND to gastric sleeve. I watched two women talk about their journeys with the LAP-BAND and what made them get revisions. They also spoke about how well they were doing now. They seemed to have lost a significant amount of weight after having their revisions done. I had spoken with my doctor numerous times in the last year about having a revision done, and he told me that it would take nearly a year for my insurance to approve it. I didn't have that kind of time. I wanted it done now.

I researched more about having revisions done. If I went to another hospital, the process would start all over from the beginning. I wanted this weight off now. I joined all sorts of blogs online under different sites for all kinds of weight-loss surgeries. I read the different postings on each surgery. I found one woman who spoke about how she went to Mexico for surgery. I thought she was crazy, but I was amazed at the results. Considering the things I had heard about weird things happening to patients in foreign countries, and here she had risked her life to go to Mexico. Wow, she must be really crazy or desperate. Then I thought, *Well, things must have been good if she was video blogging about it, and things seem okay with her.* I contacted her, and we spoke about what made her go to Mexico to have the surgery. She

Pushing Through

told me she did tons of research and it seemed very safe. She told me which doctor she used as well. I also had conversations with another woman, and she told me about her experience with getting a revision done in Mexico. She gave me her doctor's information as well. I was also on a lot of weight-loss blogging sites gaining great information on doctors.

When I logged on to specific topics, I read each comment from people who have had experiences with each surgery. I found a topic on having weight-loss surgery outside of the United States, and I subscribed to that specific topic as I wanted to read everything that went on in that forum. I started doing research on one doctor that the one woman had told me about, and found out that he charged five thousand U.S. dollars. That price seemed reasonable to me, so I started researching his clinic, him as a doctor, and anything I could find online about him. I even called the clinic to ask as many questions as I could. I spoke with my fiancée about it, and she was very skeptical about me going to Mexico for the surgery. I made sure not to tell my family about it because if my fiancée was skeptical, I know my family and friends would flip out on me. They didn't want me to have my LAP-BAND surgery, so a revision in Mexico would be out of the question. They would try their hardest to discourage me from going. Keep in mind, I wasn't going to Cancun, or any exotic island to have surgery, I was going to Tijuana. I felt pretty good about picking the one doctor, so I sent my down payment of three thousand dollars and had my time and date set for January 11, 2012, at 10:00 a.m. I was scheduled to have my LAP-BAND removed and have the gastric sleeve done.

Charise Marie

I got on the blogging sites and posted that I was excited to have scheduled my surgery and finally get the weight off. I told Tiny about it, and I had to rush because I had to pay, get both of our passports, and schedule time off from work. She was already off work on holiday leave, so she was fine to travel with me. I was excited as this surgery was to occur three days after my birthday. What a great way to celebrate every year: my birthday and surgery date around the same time!

Days after I posted the message on the blogging sites, I received a private message from another lady on the site. She told me not to go to that specific doctor because he was known to use unclean surgical instruments. She claimed that he even left gauze and other things inside of people. She left me a link that led to a post about how bad this doctor was and to stay away from him. I thanked her and said that I would review the comments. She just kept repeating that I should look for another doctor. She even told me to join specific forums on specific doctors in Mexico, so I did and thanked her again.

When she gave me this information, I was a little taken aback. I thought to myself, *Does she hate this doctor and want to tarnish his name? Does she work for another doctor and want me to go to him? Was this all real?*

If this was real, I would be crushed as I had just paid for and booked our plane tickets, scheduled time off from work, and gave that doctor the down payment. I started to freak out while reading comments about how bad the doctor was. I felt really badly as I had done lots of research on this doctor. How could I have missed this post about him?

Pushing Through

Oh my gosh, am I going to die? Will he leave things in me? Will he use dirty surgical instruments on me too?

I was terrified. To make myself feel better, I took to my video blogging page and posted a message. I asked anyone who knew of any great doctors to get information about them, and I asked them to please respond with their name. I was clearly upset in this video as most of my watchers could see. I received private messages telling me to check out two specific doctors. I gave those names to the lady who had informed me about the first doctor, and she said that she had heard all good things about them. I then researched as much information as I could on every site where each doctor's name appeared. I was not going to book with another doctor and then hear that he was not the one with whom to trust my life.

I found all kinds of great information about one of the doctors. I called his weight-loss clinic and spoke with his nurse and I told her my story. I told her that I had already booked airline tickets and had given a deposit. I asked whether there was any way they could schedule me or squeeze me in for that date. She told me that I was pushing it kind of close to the date, but she would speak with the doctor and call me back. She called me back later that night and said that I could come on that day. She explained that normally the doctor asks for his patients to stay one extra day for observation, but since I already booked our plane tickets that he would see if he could squeeze me in first thing the morning of January 11th. I thanked her at least a million times. I asked her how much I needed for a deposit and found out that I could submit as much as I could until I was able to get the refund back from the previous doctor. I

Charise Marie

sent her $1,500 and told her that as soon as I got my other money back I would send that as well. She told me not to worry. I could bring the rest in a certified check on the day I arrived for surgery.

    I was glad about that, but the only problem was that this doctor was $1,200 more than the other doctor. I panicked for a minute, but then told my fiancée and my son that Christmas was not going to be like it had been the last few years. I had to pinch every penny I earned to come up with the extra money. They both seemed to understand; at least they didn't say anything about it to my face. Keep in mind that Christmas was only eleven days away, so whatever I had already purchased was what they were going to get. Feeling a little bit more at ease, I called the previous doctor and made up a lie about not being able to get off from work. They asked whether I wanted to reschedule, and I told them that I would call at a later time when my boss allowed me that much time off. They simply said okay and wished me well in the future. I kindly said thank you and hung up really fast. I received my three thousand dollars within a day or two.

Pushing Through

"Don't quit. Suffer now and live the rest of your life as a champion." – Muhammad Ali

Charise Marie
Chapter Five: Starting Over

January 2012

My fiancée Tiny and I decided to go to Atlantic City to relax for my birthday and to prepare for my surgery. I was on a strict diet, as I was not allowed any solid foods two weeks prior to my surgery. I thought doing the two-week liquid diet before was bad, but this doctor said a liquid diet one week before this revision surgery. I did my best to try for two weeks and did rather well. I knew that the last week was going to be the hardest week, and it was. I couldn't have any cake for my birthday or eat any of the delicious foods at any of the restaurants. So, we just relaxed and played the slot machines.

We left for California early that afternoon the day before the surgery. Once we arrived, the medical team had someone pick us up and take us over the border into Tijuana, Mexico. He took us straight to the hotel where we would be staying for a few days. We looked at each other and laughed when we got there. It was a casino hotel. We loved going to casinos to stay and play, not to mention that we had just left one. We checked in, they took my bags up to my room, and then gave me food vouchers so I could sip on broth (which is what I was to have leading up to my surgery). Tiny was on her own when it came to food. I paid for everything

Pushing Through

else, so she had to at least help out and pay for her own food. My package included medicine and unlimited Jell-O, broth, and soup at the hotel.

We began playing soon after checking in, having a good time while learning their casino ways. Things were not much different from the casinos we visited in the States. The only thing different in Tijuana was that we had to take the amount of money we wanted to play with to a cashier, and she printed it out with a code on a sheet of paper. Once we got to the machine, we entered the code and the amount of money we gave her popped up on the screen. When we were finished playing, we went upstairs to bed. We needed rest for my revision surgery the next day.

We were picked up fairly early in the morning and taken over to the hospital. I completed some paperwork, and then they drew blood and asked multiple questions. Most nurses back in the States had a hard time drawing my blood; this nurse, however, went right in and had blood as soon as she pricked me. I laughed in amazement by how quickly she got blood from my vein. They took me to the back and I kissed my fiancée Tiny and we said a prayer together. I met the doctor once I was in the back. He was very nice and polite and answered all the questions I had. He asked me if I wanted my LAP-BAND once he took it out. I laughed. He said most people wanted it, so I agreed to take it. They took me down for surgery, and the next thing I knew I was waking up in the recovery room. They later took me to my actual room where I saw my fiancée after I was done in the recovery room. Tiny kept in touch with my family back home, letting them know how things were going with me. We all were scared, but my family probably was more

Charise Marie

scared than I was.

Once I was awake, I started walking, and I filmed my entire process so I could upload it on my video blog. I saw the doctor that evening. He told me that everything went well. There was a lot of scarring around my LAP-BAND, but that was to be expected, he explained. He said, "You should feel gassy but no other pain other than that. I want to monitor you for a few more days just to make sure you are okay." I thanked him. He then turned around and said that he had a present for me and gave me my LAP-BAND in a plastic surgical bag. I laughed and said, "Thanks for everything." He told me to call with questions, no matter what.

I stayed in the hospital for two days, and once discharged, spent another two days at the hotel. The doctor's medical team gave me all the things I needed to take back to the hotel room: bottled water, pain medication, juices, gauze, and a few other things. Once we arrived back at the hotel, I went downstairs to play in the casino. My social media friends told me to go upstairs to my room and rest. I laughed and told them that I wasn't in any pain. Most of them knew this to be true as they had had surgery as well. They knew the minimal amount of pain that came with the surgery. Not all experienced minimal pain, though; some people had had a lot of pain and some had had none. I was fortunate enough not to have much pain. I just had a lot of discomfort, which they say is gas because they pump air into your stomach during the surgery.

I walked around the casino to avoid getting blood clots. One isn't supposed to lie around after these kinds of surgeries.

Pushing Through

Tiny and I took pictures and did a little sightseeing in Tijuana. We didn't go too far as we didn't know where we were. We did have the chance to meet Tijuana's soccer team, though. We knew they were big-time people as they had on jerseys and everyone was very excited when they saw them come in the door. So, I walked over and politely asked who they were, and one guy laughed and said, "Where are you from?" I told him Philadelphia, and he said, "Oh, great." He told me that he was a part of the soccer team. I asked for a picture, so he rounded up the guys for a picture with me.

Once we arrived home, I was on leave from work for another two weeks. My fiancée went back to work that Monday. I did pretty well at home; I couldn't work out, of course. I could only start up again six weeks after surgery. I followed everything on the list that the doctor and nutritionist gave me. It included much of the same things I had had when I had the LAP-BAND: broths, clear juices, soft boiled eggs, yogurt, tuna, and other soft foods. The funny thing was that I scrambled one egg and tried to eat it but could only eat two-thirds. When I boiled an egg, I could not get even half of it down. I was pretty frustrated in the beginning of the process because I couldn't eat like I wanted to, but I knew that that was the point: to change my eating habits and not eat as much.

Before I knew it, I had lost weight and was so happy. Tiny was amazed by how much I had lost. I had weighed 284 pounds when I arrived in Mexico, and that was from working out pretty hard in the gym three to four times a week. I was very proud of my starting weight before this surgery. Keep in mind that my highest weight was 344 pounds. I was a huge Butterball turkey. By the time the next weight-loss convention came around, I was close to 230 pounds.

January 2013

I did my first weight-loss anniversary blogging video telling everyone how my year had gone since my revision surgery. I recorded the video under the name "Ms-Mook1979." My lowest weight was 209 pounds and I was wearing size fourteen. I also did an all-picture video, showing all the pictures I had taken for the past year. I was able to walk in most stores and see that they had my size; I was able to fit in the plane seats without asking for a seat belt extender. I could even fit in knee boots! I wore a dress for my birthday party. I hadn't worn a dress in years and it felt really good, but it was pretty weird at the same time. I received so many compliments about how good I looked in that dress.

Pushing Through

"Life is 10% what happens to us and 90% how we react to it." – Dennis P. Kimbro

Charise Marie
Chapter Six:
Baby Fever

April 2013

    My fiancée Tiny and I decided that we wanted to have a baby of our own. When we first got into a relationship, I made it known to her that having a baby was something I wanted to do, God willing. She wanted to adopt but claimed she was open to the idea of having a newborn. I think she wanted to change my mind about getting pregnant, but I kept telling her that I wanted to have my own child first. I wanted to at least try a few times to get pregnant before I looked into adoption.

    She finally came on board with us having a baby, but she told me that she thought a brand-new baby would impede our lifestyle. I told her that we'd have plenty of babysitters, and we laughed. The first thing Tiny and I sat down and talked about was how we were going to get the sperm. We discussed and both agreed that me lying with a man was not an option. We knew she didn't have any brothers to keep her blood line attached to the baby so that was out of the question. She asked did I want her coworker to shoot the sperm in the cup and I told her no I didn't feel comfortable with him. We would need to draw up papers stating he is dropping all parental rights to our baby. I told her I think its best we go with an unknown sperm donor and just go

Pushing Through

with a sperm bank.

So, I started doing research on how lesbians could have babies without a male figure in the household. Most people thought the process was different for a lesbian to have a baby without a man, but, if you really thought about it, it was the same process. An egg and a sperm meet and voilà! The only difference was that with having two females, one would need to be inseminated with the sperm from a sperm bank or a close male figure in her life.

I found a lot of sperm banks and fertility clinics during my research. I heard a few people talk about the turkey baster method—when you put the sperm in a syringe or turkey baster and insert it into your vagina. It's a lot more complicated than that, however. I went online to search for ways to get pregnant at home with insemination kits. I also joined plenty of lesbian trying-to-conceive (TTC) groups on social media. I told my mom that I was thinking of having a baby, and she said, "You don't need any babies, girl, the one you have is all you need." I told a few of my close friends that I wanted to have a baby, and they all thought I was crazy because my son would be eighteen soon and out of the home.

I just shrugged off all their comments, and although they hurt, I didn't respond to any of them. I decided that when and if we do start trying, that I wouldn't tell anyone until I was due. I thought that people, especially my family and friends, would be supportive. Even if they didn't think it was a good idea, at least they could say that they supported me. But no, not my family and friends. They thought I didn't need another child. It kind of made me feel like I'm a

Charise Marie

bad mother or something.

May 2013

I told Tiny that we didn't have money to go to a fertility clinic because most of them in our area were $15,000 or more. We decided to do the home-insemination method described in the groups online. I picked out an at-home insemination kit and a sperm donor from a very popular sperm bank. It was very expensive for the sperm, almost eight hundred dollars. We liked this sperm bank because it sent sperm to our home without the permission of a fertility doctor or clinic. We received the kit and followed all the directions. We took the sperm out of the huge container it came in and let it get room temperature. We then inserted the sperm into the syringe and put it into my vagina. I had my legs up in the air like a fool for twenty to thirty minutes, thinking it would help the sperm travel. Two weeks later, which was the time they tell you to check to see if you are pregnant, I found out that I was not pregnant. I was devastated, to say the least.

I posted the following on social media:

Got some bad news. Feeling like crying. Really feeling sad right now. I know God has my back. It will work out in the end.

After being devastated about not being pregnant in May, my best friend Heaven told me that she didn't want to see me hurt and crying. She said that she didn't know what I was feeling, but that she'd have the baby for me. I cried and asked her if she would. She said yes. I thanked Heaven and told her that I would consider the offer. I was very happy

Pushing Through

to hear her say that she would carry my baby. There was no way I would have her do that for me, however, especially since she already had four kids of her own. How would we explain it to her children? Besides that, I wanted to experience pregnancy again myself. I wanted to feel the kicks and the movements; I wanted to wonder whether it was a boy or girl. Although I never experienced morning sickness with my son, I wanted all the things that come with being a mother, even the weight gain, swollen feet, and penguin waddle. Getting pregnant again was one of the reasons I had weight-loss surgery.

June 2013

My best friend Heaven called and said, "I know it's been a month since the pregnancy test said negative, and I know you really want to have a baby. Have you ever considered adoption?"

I said, "I have, but I want to explore options for having my own baby first. But I do want to adopt. There are a lot of children who need a loving home, but I want to try myself a few times first."

"My sister is pregnant," she said, "and she wants to give the baby up. She and her boyfriend want to finish college and want to give their child up for adoption."

"Oh wow, that sounds great."

She said, "My family knows you, and I'm sure you can come up with some kind of agreement between the three of you."

Charise Marie

I said, "We definitely need to come to some kind of agreement because I don't want them to sign the baby over to me and then want the baby back after I raised it for a few months or years."

"I will get in touch with my sister to see what she wants to do."

After a few weeks she informed me that her sister would be giving the baby to her sixty-year-old aunt to raise. I was a little hurt, but I tried not to let it get me down. I tried not to get my hopes up too high only to be hurt again.

Sept 2013

I had saved my income tax refunds for two years. I also had been having my job place money into two of my five bank accounts. I wanted to make sure that when the time came that I would have enough money saved to not only raise a baby but to go to a fertility clinic, if needed. Now I'm not saying I had $20,000 lying around, but I am a saving queen. My fiancée Tiny has never been good with saving money, so I couldn't rely on her when it came to money.

I researched fertility clinics in my area and found some. Then I started researching the doctors of the fertility clinics that I found. Most were very pricey, but that was something I expected. I decided on one particular fertility clinic because it was close to my job, which was very convenient. I picked a female doctor to be my reproductive endocrinologist.

I went to visit her for all my blood work in October.

Pushing Through

She explained the procedures and the prices. I was a little skeptical, but I figured that she would be able to help me achieve the goal of having a baby. I have one child now, so why would it be difficult to conceive another? All of my blood tests came back fine. I told her how I had tried to get pregnant back in May. She told me that I may have done something wrong. She told me to purchase some ovulation strips or kits online or in the local department store and instructed me to start using them right after my menstrual cycle came.

I went home and researched sperm banks in my area. The first sperm bank I used was extremely expensive. Paying eight hundred dollars for one vial of sperm is absolutely ridiculous to me, especially if you don't get pregnant. All that money just goes down the drain. I had to find a place that would ship sperm to my home or to the clinic. I found one place that had great prices. The only problem was that they didn't have many choices of African-American men. They had two men who were close to my needs. One of them I just knew was not the right one for me. The second guy had more than one ethnicity. His mother was British and German, and his father was African American and Native American I didn't mind him as he was the closest match to what I wanted. His sperm had produced multiple babies, and this sperm bank had the cheapest sperm vials, so he was my chosen donor.

I went into the fertility clinic and did all my testing and blood work. My doctor told me to start using my ovulation strips to indicate when I was ovulating.

Charise Marie

November 2013

I got the first positive ovulation strip the day before Thanksgiving. I was excited. I had woken up Thanksgiving morning and had to wait to test until the second time I had to urinate. I anxiously awaited while I drank water to make myself have to go to the bathroom. Boom, I had to use the bathroom again. Yes!

I ran into the bathroom, used the ovulation strip, and yes, it was positive. I called the reproductive endocrinologist and let her know. She told me that I could come in around 1:00 p.m., but that they were in another city that day. I was a little upset that they were further outside of our city, and on Thanksgiving, but I was willing to travel to the end of this Earth just to get pregnant and have another child. I wanted to be a mommy again really badly. I have so much love inside of me to give to another child. I was ready!

Tiny and I arrived in her office. My doctor wasn't there and I was pissed. They had me see one of her colleagues who practiced in her office. He asked me when he came to see me if I had identified my sperm donor's sperm as the correct number I had purchased. I said yes. He sat down and prepped me about what he was going to do, then told me to undress from the waist down, lie back, and relax. He came back in the room with the nurse, asked one more time about the sperm, and then told me to relax again. I held my fiancée's hand and the doctor inserted the sperm.

When he was done, he asked if I had any questions, and, of course, I did. He told me to lie there for twenty minutes before getting dressed and going to the front desk for more

Pushing Through

paperwork.

    I still had my fiancée's hand so we squeezed each other's hands. We said a prayer. I was in a little bit of pain, so the doctor told me to take two Tylenols and I should be fine.

    We stopped at a department store and picked up a cheap little blanket to take to my parents' house for Thanksgiving so we could sit, eat, and enjoy family. We got there and everyone asked what took us so long. I basically said that I was in a little pain, but that I was okay. The only people who knew I was inseminated were Tiny and my cousin. My cousin asked how everything went, and I told her that everything was fine. I let her know that I was in a bit of pain and that I would be spotting for a few days.

    We enjoyed the rest of Thanksgiving with the family and then went home. When we got there, I laid on my fiancée's shoulder and we said another prayer that this insemination worked. I was hurt when the first didn't work, so I think I said a million extra prayers over the next two weeks. The reproductive endocrinologist told me to wait thirteen to sixteen days after the insemination before taking a pregnancy test. I had no patience so I tested on the twelfth day. The result? A big, fat negative. I had purchased a bunch of ovulation strips and pregnancy tests so I could test for at least eight or nine days. I tested on days thirteen, fourteen, and fifteen, and yet again, had big, fat negatives. I said a bigger prayer on day sixteen and took the test. Another negative. I just cried in the bathroom. I thought that maybe I just couldn't have any more kids or something. Why me? I'm a good person. I'm a good mom. Why me? Why me?

Charise Marie

I went on with the holidays—Christmas, New Year's and my birthday—like I wasn't hurting inside. I was hoping, wishing, and praying to give birth again. This was the second time that my insemination had failed. I didn't want to be devastated again. My fiancée and I had an argument and we both said things we didn't mean. I told her that the one thing that stuck out about that argument was when she said, "That's why God don't bless no mess; this is why you're going through what you're going through now." I was devastated by that comment. I told her that I would never be able to forgive her. Just because we had some bad times in our relationship didn't mean that God shouldn't bless me with a child. I resented her for that statement throughout our entire relationship.

Pushing Through

"Not every day is a good day, live anyway."

– Unknown

Charise Marie
Chapter Seven:
The Worst Day of My Life

April 2014

My friends and I would always sit around and chat, go to the movies and dinner, and take trips too. So, I suggested we go out and start volunteering to give back to the community. Everyone agreed and thought it was a great idea. I told them that I would put some stuff together over the next few days and present the ideas to them the next time we saw each other.

I came up with a name for our new non-profit organization: Great Services Association. We now had our first volunteer event planned for the month of May. We would cook breakfast for forty to fifty families living in a local house. This house held families with children who were in the hospital with serious illnesses. We were very excited for our first event. It made us all feel very good to be able to help people who rarely got home-cooked meals while away from their homes and worrying about their children.

It was around this time that my fiancée and I spoke about me trying to get pregnant again. I was a little apprehensive about it for a while. But then I decided that I would

Pushing Through

try again after I saved up more money.

I got a phone call on April 8th from my dad telling me that my grandmother passed away early that morning. I was hurt, but I realized that we had repaired our relationship over the last ten to twelve years and now God needed her more than I did. He needed his angel back. I had thirty-five years with her so I was blessed to have her for that long.

The day after my grandmother died, I got to work and my coworkers, who knew that my grandmother had passed, asked what I was doing there. I said that I couldn't sit home doing nothing but cry. Besides, we only got one day off for the Family and Medical Leave Act (FMLA), so I would use one for the day before and one vacation day for the day of the funeral if it was on a weekday. Then my coworker said she found out human resources were doing a big layoff that day at our job. I worked as a Junior Data Manager for a non-profit organization for cancer patients.

I prayed: *Please God, not today. Not today. I've been here eight years and don't want to lose my job after losing my grandmother yesterday. I can't deal with two losses back to back, God.*

I found out that they were calling people on their desk phones every twenty to thirty minutes, so any time one of our phones rang, we all looked at the phone like *please don't let it be me.* So many people were laid off that day. Thirty was the number we were told. These were people who had been with the company for years.

Charise Marie

The layoff that hit me the hardest was a coworker with whom I was really close. She was an older woman in her early seventies, and we talked like we were grandmother and granddaughter. Regardless of race (she is white, and I am black), I viewed her as my grandmother. When she told me that she was one of the people getting laid off, I burst into tears. She said, "I'm getting up there in age; no need to cry because I'm getting laid off."

I said, "I know, but it feels like another loss. I lost my grandmother yesterday to death and now I'm losing you to a layoff, and you're like a grandmother to me."

She gave me her condolences and said, "You will be just fine. Besides, it's time for me to go back to my retirement again."

The rest of the work day was sad as we learned about all the people who were let go. At the same time, however, I was thanking God that I was not called in to be laid off.

By the end of April, I started thinking about trying again for another baby.

I contacted the same sperm bank because my donor's sperm had worked; it just hadn't worked with me. I explained to them that I would be returning soon.

Pushing Through

May 2014

I contacted my reproductive endocrinologist and told her that I wanted to try again. She said great, and I started counting my ovulation days with the ovulating strips I had left. She also told me that she wanted me to try some low-dose fertility medications. She gave me a medication to increase my chances of getting pregnant. I started taking it at the end of May, early June.

I ordered my sperm and had it shipped to her so it would be in the clinic if I did start ovulating. I tested for about a week and a half, and on June 30th, I got a light-pink positive on the ovulation strip. I called my fertility clinic and they told me to give it one more day to see if the pink got darker. I waited one more day. On July 1st, it was a dark pink line. I was ecstatic!

July 2014

They scheduled me to come in at 1:00 p.m. that day to be inseminated. My fiancée Tiny had to work, unfortunately, so she was unable to go with me to the clinic. I called her and texted her, filling her in with everything that was going on. They called me into the back to review my information and the sperm that was sent. Everything was in order. They made me check if the sperm donor's number was correct. It was.

The doctor had me lie on the table where I said a million prayers. He inserted the sperm into my vagina and told me to lie there for twenty minutes before putting my bottoms back on and seeing them at the front desk. I laid there and

Charise Marie

all I did was pray, pray, pray.

Please God, I've wanted to have another child these last ten or fifteen years, and I know my son always wanted to have a baby brother or sister. Please help me accomplish this. I'm willing to give up anything just to get pregnant. God, please. Oh, and God, before I go, I will give up cereal. I will not eat cereal for nine whole months.

I know I made God laugh with that prayer. Anyone who knows me knows that I am a cereal freak. I eat cereal up to seven times a week. So, telling God that I would give up cereal in order to be pregnant was pretty huge. I left the clinic and called my fiancée and told her what happened and we said a prayer over the phone. After a while, I got home and rested. I prayed and cried and cried and prayed that the insemination would work this time. My fertility doctor told me to test for pregnancy twelve to sixteen days after insemination.

July 15th came, two weeks from the day of insemination. I used a pregnancy test and pregnancy strip and they were confusing. The pregnancy test was negative but the pregnancy strip was light pink. I was confused, but I was also optimistic that this third try with intrauterine insemination (IUI) would be our lucky chance. They say third time's the charm, right?

July 16th came and my fiancée said she was on her way to pick me up from home. We were going to support a friend at her softball game. I tested with the strip earlier at work and it was dark pink, which meant I was pregnant, but I needed to confirm with more than one test. I had experienced too

Pushing Through

much disappointment to get my hopes up. I quickly ran to the bathroom and used a pregnancy test, but turned it face down. My fiancée called me and I told her I was ready at the door. I lied because I was sitting in the bathroom waiting for the pregnancy test results.

Without checking the test again, I hurried up, washed my hands, and left to attend the softball game.

We arrived back home later and my fiancée had to use the bathroom. I was in the kitchen putting stuff in the refrigerator when she screamed down the stairs for me.

"Babe! Babe! Oh my gosh, Babe!" I became frantic thinking that something had happened to her or worse, something was broken in the bathroom and was going to cost a billion dollars to fix. I said, "What's wrong?"

She screamed, "It's positive! It's positive! Get up here!"

I was like, "What is she talking about?"

She came running down the stairs and shoved the pregnancy test in my face. She said, "Look! It's positive!"

I said, "WHAT! Oh my gosh!" I got a little teary.

I immediately said, "Please God, let this be true. Please God, I beg you. I told you I would give up cereal the entire nine months. Please, God, please!"

She grabbed me and we hugged and said the third time was the charm. I said, "Let's not get too happy yet. I need

Charise Marie

to really make sure we are pregnant before we get all slap happy telling the world."

I was at work the next day and told one coworker, who knew I was trying, that the test came back positive. She congratulated me. I told her that I really didn't want to get my hopes up too high just yet because it's still early.

I went in the bathroom stall at my job and took another pregnancy strip and test just to see if yesterday's test was true. Lo and behold, they were both showing positive signs. I don't know how long I stayed in that stall, but I stayed in there just crying and thanking God that those tests came out positive. I couldn't stop crying happy tears and saying happy prayers.

I got back to my desk and told my coworker that those tests were positive as well. I said, "I'm calling the fertility clinic to make an appointment for tomorrow." The clinic asked about my results and then told me to come in for a blood and urine test the next day.

I took my little cousin to dinner that evening for her birthday, just the two of us. I kind of told her a little bit about my day, but didn't say that I was pregnant. She said if I did get pregnant, she would be so happy for me.

The morning of July 18th I took the test at my fertility clinic and the urine test showed I was pregnant. The nurse congratulated me. She said, "Are you excited?"

I said, "I am now that it's confirmed." I texted Tiny and told her it was true. I told my coworker as well. She said that

Pushing Through

she was excited for me.

I tried so hard not to tell anyone, and I made my fiancée promise that she wouldn't tell anyone either. She asked why she couldn't, and I told her that I didn't want to jinx anything. I've been told over the years not to announce pregnancy until after three months in case something happens.

We were very excited, but I kept trying to hold back because I wanted to wait until I was on the delivery table before I told anyone. I just kept getting an eerie feeling.

We met with my non-profit organization the next day; we were having a clothing drive out in the park. Two of our friends, Irene and Nicole but we called her Nic for short, asked how we were, and we looked at them and gave a nod to each other because there was no way we were really going to keep our mouths shut. After all, it was great news, something we had been wanting for quite some time. I looked at our friends and said, "I have something to tell you guys. I'm happy and excited, but I really don't want to tell you because I really don't want to jinx it. But I can't hold it in. I found out I was pregnant a few days ago." They seemed ecstatic! I said, "Please don't tell anyone yet. I'm trying to keep it hush-hush for a while." They agreed, and hugged me with excitement.

Two of my other friends, Kelly and Theresa, showed up a few hours later, and, of course, I told them the good news too. They were excited for us as well.

Then I told one of my coworkers who was laid off from

my work and he was so happy. He told me that he was going to start purchasing some baby onesies. I immediately told him not to until I was five or six months pregnant.

My fiancée and I started looking up baby registries and decided to do a few. I was skeptical about doing one, but still excited. We found out we were due March 22nd, 2015.

Thursday, July 24th

I went to my fertility clinic to get my first ultrasound and have more blood work done. My doctor told me during my ultrasound that she could not locate the baby. She warned me that there may be something wrong, that I had to come back Monday for another ultrasound, and that she would take it from there.

I started to panic after I got up from her table.

I got to work and told my coworker. She said not to think the worst. I immediately jumped on baby- blogging sites and the majority of the women on them said not to panic; it's way too early to see a baby. The babies are the size of mustard seeds, after all, so give it more time. I told my fiancée about it and she said to pray. I told her that the people on the sites said it may be too early, and she said, "It may be, babe; stop panicking. Everything will be fine."

Pushing Through

Friday, July 25th

We got up pretty early; I had taken off work that day. My fiancée and I were going to Delaware because our friends were getting married that evening on the beach. We packed and got on the road around noon.

As we were driving, my fiancée said, "I know you're going crazy with the doctor saying that she didn't see the baby, but we have to keep praying all is well."

I said, "Yes, I know. I'm going to just hope that it's too soon to see the baby. I do feel, though, that since she is a fertility doctor, she should already know when to schedule my appointment to see my baby through the ultrasound."

"Yes, she should." My fiancée continued, "Talk to me as I'm driving. Let's think of more baby names. Read me the list of girl and boy names we came up with plus the rest you added."

I told her the names we both came up with, the new names I had added, and we even decided the names we wanted once the boy or girl arrived. I joked with her and said, "Oh babe, what if we have twins?"

She said, "Please don't make me crash," and we laughed.

"No seriously, what if God blesses us with twins? Remember I was on that fertility medication that can make

Charise Marie

me produce more than one egg."

She said, "That's not funny, but we will embrace it if it's true."

I said, "We would have no choice but to embrace it. So, let's think of twin names for boys, girls, and a boy and a girl." We started by saying different names for twin boys that rhymed, then twin girls that rhymed.

I said, "Well I guess this means we need to start thinking of boy and girl twin names too." So, we thought of those and I wrote down all the names in my notes section on my phone.

We arrived in Dover, Delaware, and went to our hotel. The receptionist told us that it was too early to check in.

We put down our stuff in the lobby. We had packed some sandwiches and salads to eat before the wedding reception that evening. I started to feel a light pain in my stomach, so I asked the lady where the bathroom was and she showed me. I thought I just had pain from holding my bladder, but I was worried. I started saying a prayer, hoping everything was okay with the baby.

We sat in the lobby area where they serve breakfast, and we ate our food while watching a little bit of television. I told Tiny that I had had a pain in my stomach and that I didn't know where it was coming from. I was scared because the doctor said she couldn't find the baby, so that thought stayed on my mind constantly. We held hands over the table and said a prayer. The pain started to get worse

Pushing Through

and I got really scared. I told the lady that I really needed to get into the room because I was in a lot of pain and had just found out I was pregnant. She told me to hold on to see what she could do. She then told me she would have to charge me an extra seventy-five to one hundred dollars for early check in. I walked away and laid down on the couch in the lobby area because I was pissed off. Check-in was at 3:00 p.m. and it was around 2:30 or so.

I called the fertility doctor's office and spoke with the nurse. I told her that I was having pains in my stomach. She spoke with the doctor and then asked if I could come in to be checked. She believed I may be pregnant in my tube, which is why she couldn't find the embryo on Thursday. What! She didn't tell me about the possibility of being pregnant in my tube when I was there. She just said they couldn't find the baby as of yet but to come back on Monday. I told her I was out of town for a wedding. I asked if I could take a Tylenol to subdue the pain and she said yes, but if the pain got worse to go to the nearest hospital.

The lady in the hotel finally cleared us to go up to our room.

I collapsed on the bed as soon as I got there because I was in so much pain. I laid balled up like a baby in the fetal position. My fiancée asked if I was okay, and I just said, "No, I'm in a lot of pain." She got up and got dressed for the wedding as I nodded off. She then woke me up from my nap to get dressed. I hesitated for a minute because I was in so much pain. All I cared about at that moment was making sure my baby was okay. My fiancée tried to convince me that because we had come all that way we needed to hurry

Charise Marie

and head over to Rehoboth Beach for the wedding.

Now I was getting pissed off with her. I yelled and told her that she didn't care anything about me or the baby. She said, "That's not true, but we didn't come all the way over here to lie in the room. We came over here for a wedding." I got up and called the doctor, and she told me to go to the nearest hospital if the pain came back and the Tylenol didn't work. She told me that she believed I was pregnant in my tube but still wanted to see me on Monday morning. She asked if I would be back by then and I told her I would. We were only in Delaware for the night because on Saturday my non-profit organization was volunteering at a place where they package food to give to those in need.

I got dressed and we left. I made my fiancée take me to the convenience store up the street to get more Tylenol and I took two pills. I texted a handful of my friends, the few who knew I was pregnant, asking them to pray for me as I was in excruciating pain. My friends were really angry about the fact that I was going to the wedding and not the hospital. I told one friend, Irene, that I just stopped to get some Tylenol for the pain and she said I should take my ass to the hospital. I told her that my fiancée really wanted to go to the wedding and she said to forget the wedding; something could be happening to the baby. Had I talked to my doctor? I said, "Yeah, she told me to go to the hospital if the pain gets worse."

We arrived at the beach and walked over to the area where the wedding was taking place. I still had pain, but it was diminishing some. I guess the Tylenol was working. We sat on the chairs that were placed out for the wedding and

Pushing Through

spoke to a lot of people we knew. The wedding began and my pain wasn't too bad, I guess because I took the Tylenol. It helped out a lot, but not as much as I thought. The pain felt like I had just drunk three gallons of water and like I needed to go to the bathroom; it was very uncomfortable.

The wedding and the couple was beautiful, and we were happy to share in their happy day. As we left, I checked my phone and saw that I had more messages from my friends screaming at me about needing to go to the hospital. I told them that my fiancée was hungry so we were going to try and head all the way over to Lewes, Delaware, where the reception was located. My friends were mad at me because we didn't go straight to the hospital but told me to keep them posted.

The pain started coming back even stronger once we arrived at the reception. I told my fiancée that we had to give our congratulations and then find the nearest hospital. She seemed mad at me because she was hungry. I got very frustrated with her and said that I was ready to go to the hospital. She, however, was ready to mingle, eat, and dance. I looked at her and said that something could be wrong with our baby; the doctor told me I might be pregnant in my tube. My fiancée finally said that we would leave after the couple arrived.

I searched online for a hospital in the area and one was a few blocks from our hotel room all the way back in Dover. We arrived at the hospital after a long drive. My fiancée posted on social media asking for prayers as we entered the hospital. I was checked in quickly. I said a prayer: *God, please do not let this be my baby, please.*

Charise Marie

I told them that I just found out I was pregnant, so they took my vitals, asked for a urine sample, and drew my blood. The nurse then told me that they were going to give me a large cup that could be refilled with ice and water, and to drink as much as I could. They would be doing an ultrasound and my bladder needed to be full.

The ultrasound technician asked me a bunch of questions. She inserted the transducer wand into my vaginal area so she could see inside; a transvaginal ultrasound is what they called it. I started asking questions, and she told me that she couldn't tell me what was going on. All she does is take the pictures, she explained, and the doctor would read me the results. She then took the wand out of me and did an abdominal ultrasound. This took all of about twenty minutes to do. She then left for ten minutes and came back and said I needed to drink more water because they weren't getting a clear picture. I was frustrated at this point but was still praying that the pain I was feeling was from eating bad food or something. She came back in and repeated the whole procedure. After she was finished, she left to get the doctor. He came in and asked about my pain level. I told him it was a twenty. He then explained that he was going to repeat the procedure again. I was getting extremely pissed now. He put the wand in me and moved it all around. Not only was it uncomfortable, but it was beginning to hurt.

As I was lying there, flinching, I prayed *please not my baby, please not my baby*. That's all I kept repeating over and over. He took out the wand, did the abdominal ultrasound, and then stuck two fingers in me. This was the seventh time I had had ultrasounds and I wanted answers right then.

Pushing Through

This whole thing took a little over an hour.

The nurses got me back to my room where the female doctor came in to give me the results. I dreaded hearing the words I knew she was going to say.

She said, "I'm sorry to say this but you are pregnant in your left tube." She said, "You will lose your baby, but there is a possibility, depending on the damage done to your tube, that we will be able to save your tube. The good thing is, even if we are unable to save your left tube, you can always try and get pregnant again with your right tube."

I just cried and couldn't stop. I was losing my baby. I cried so hard and hurt so bad inside. I would never wish this pain on my worst enemy.

The doctor told me that I had the option of taking a pill that would dissolve the baby in my tube, or I could have surgery. She also stated that they had called one of the best doctors they had at the hospital. He would be in soon as she was about to be off duty. He would explain anything else that I had questions about.

I thanked her, put my head down, and cried. My fiancée Tiny then started crying as she saw me in so much pain. I looked at her and said, "Do you realize we are about to lose our baby? We fought so hard to get pregnant, and now this. We found out less than ten days ago and it's been snatched away just like that. They say the third time is the charm, well this charm sucks." I could not stop crying for the life of me. It felt like someone was ripping my heart out with their bare hands.

Charise Marie

    I kept drifting in and out because of the morphine drip they gave me to help my pain go down. I laid there until the doctor arrived. He came in and asked if I had any questions. I told him that I needed him to save my baby. He told me there was no way they would be able to do that. I said, "With all the technology you guys have now days, no one has developed anything on saving babies in tubes?" He explained that I had an ectopic pregnancy, which meant I was pregnant in my tube. He asked if I wanted to have surgery. I said, "Yes, I refuse to live in this pain for days or weeks by taking some pill that will dissolve this pregnancy." He asked where my pain was, and I said that I was experiencing more pain on my right side. He said, "I'll be back. I'm going to get more information on your case."

    I had to call my mom and let her know what was going on. I was about to have major surgery and was in another state. I looked at the time and it was 3:00 a.m. I knew there was a chance that she would be up; sometimes she can't sleep through the night. I called and there was no answer, so I called my son's cell phone. He usually had his cell phone near him and would pick up. Both Tiny and I cell phone signals were intermittent, so they allowed me to call from the hospital phone in my room. I kept trying with my cell phone so he would recognize the number. See, after my mom made the comment about me not needing to have any more children, I decided not to tell her or any of my family or close friends about this pregnancy until months down the line.

    I finally got in touch with my son, and while trying not to cry on the phone, I told him that I needed to speak with his "mom mom". He said she was asleep, and I told him he

Pushing Through

had to wake her up since I was in the hospital about to have surgery. He asked what was wrong. I told him I couldn't explain it yet but I would later.

I talked to my mom and told her the whole story. I told her I would give my phone to my fiancée and have her talk to her while I was in surgery so they would know what was going on with me.

The doctor came back in and told me that I was pregnant in my left tube, and I asked, "Well then why am I feeling excruciating pain on my right side?" He couldn't explain why, other than maybe the blood from the baby had burst my tube and it's spreading to the right side, but it didn't look like that's the case by the picture. He then stated that he might have the ultrasound picture backward, viewed it again, and said, "No, it's the left side."

I said, "Okay, let's play a game, doc. If you are able to go in and save my baby, will you?"

He said, "I won't be able to save your baby; I may be able to save your tube if it's not badly damaged, but not the baby. We are not able to save babies that are stuck in fallopian tubes, Ms. Brown. I'm sorry."

"What if you go in and see that the baby is in the right tube and not the left?" I asked.

He said, "The same thing, Ms. Brown. We have to take the baby."

"Well, what if I'm pregnant with twins?"

Charise Marie

He said, "That could be possible, Ms. Brown, but this picture shows that you are pregnant in your left tube."

"But what if I'm pregnant in both of my tubes?" I questioned.

He said, "Well, Ms. Brown, I will be honest with you. In most cases in twin pregnancies with an ectopic, one normally goes through the tube and the other gets stuck. I've done multiple ectopic surgeries over the years and I have never encountered a double ectopic. I know of a colleague of mine who had a double ectopic years ago, but I've never performed any myself so you would be a first."

I said, "If I'm pregnant with twins, please wake me up and let me decide what to do. There is no way I can lose both babies."

He said, "Ms. Brown, now you know I can't do that. But things will work out for you. I will try my hardest to save your left tube. I will check back with you shortly. We will be taking you down for surgery around 7:00 a.m."

I told my fiancée to go back to our hotel room and to get some sleep and that I would call her when I was getting ready to go down for surgery. She said she didn't want to leave my side, and I told her, "I'm going to try and sleep off this morphine drip and pray that when I wake up I'll find out that this was a horrible nightmare and none of this is happening. Besides, I paid for the hotel room and it needs to be used in some kind of way."

Pushing Through

She said, "Please make sure you call me before you go down to surgery."

"I will call you. Please try to rest up some."

Saturday, July 26th

The nurse came and got me around 7:00 a.m. to take me down for surgery. I couldn't hold back my tears. I cried the entire night: every single time I woke up in pain, I just cried. I called my fiancée and told her that they would be taking me down in a few minutes, and that she should come within the next one to two hours.

I cried in the room while waiting for the doctor to come in and prep me. The nurse was standing there and she said, "I know it hurts losing your baby, but the doctor will take very good care for you." She then said, "This is never easy for me when we do these surgeries, and we do them quite often. It's never easy for the mother to lose her baby, and deep down it hurts us to see you lose your baby."

The anesthesiologist came in and asked if I was allergic to any anesthesia. "Not to my knowledge," I replied. He then told me that they were going to have me count backward and I should be out like a light. They took me into the operating room and he placed the mask over my face and told me to count down. I got to nine and that was all I remembered until I woke up in the recovery room.

I looked around the room and to my left was my fiancée Tiny sitting there with a cup of candy and a balloon that said "Get Well Soon." I looked to my right and saw the

Charise Marie

nurse coming over with some water for my dry throat. They signaled for the doctor to come over and talk to me.

"Ms. Brown, I don't know what it is about you, but you were right. You were pregnant in both of your tubes." He pulled out a paper and showed me three pictures: one where I was pregnant in both my tubes, one with the babies taken out of my tubes, and one where my tubes used to be. I had to compose myself, so I took a deep breath. I said, "So, what does this mean?"

He said, "I had to remove your tubes because they were too damaged."

"Wait a minute," I said, "let me get this straight. I was pregnant in both of my tubes, which is why you saw the baby on the left but I felt pain on the right?"

He said, "Yes, the second baby didn't show up on the ultrasound. We didn't know about the baby on the right until we went in."

Constant tears flowed down my face. I said to him, "So not only was I pregnant with one baby, but two babies, and not only did you take both babies, you took both my tubes."

He said, "Yes, Ms. Brown, I'm sorry."

"So, my chances of having a baby now are gone just like that?" I asked.

He said, "No, there is always in vitro fertilization, also known as IVF."

Pushing Through

I screamed, "I know all about IVF. Do I look like I have twenty freaking thousand dollars lying around for that?"

He said, "I understand your frustration, but your tubes were damaged. If we had left the babies in you, one or both of your tubes would have ruptured, which would have led to infection in your body that could be potentially deadly."

He gave me the pictures, his contact information, and my discharge paperwork. I looked at my fiancée and said, "I was pregnant with twins. Twins! Now we can't have kids anymore."

She said, "Babe, it's going to work out."

"How? We don't have $20,000 to have IVF; there's no possible way."

The nurse asked if I needed anything so I had her help me to the bathroom.

I sat in the bathroom and just sobbed, crying puddles and puddles of tears. I thought to myself, *I can't take this pain. I need to find the roof of this hospital and jump. I can't take this pain at all. I'm sure the nurse is gone by now since I took long enough in the bathroom, so I can go now and find the roof and jump. I just want to kill myself. All I feel like right now is dying. Why should I care anything about myself when God did this to me? He doesn't care about me so why should I care? Everything keeps happening to me and I just don't understand it. Why? I just don't understand why everything bad happens to me. From day one when I was born, God must've hated me. All the admissions to the hospitals for my asthma, not being able*

Charise Marie

to breathe, the surgery on my legs, multiple other surgeries, losing my grandparents; it is all too much for me. He doesn't love me, so why should I love myself? It makes no sense to stay here on Earth when he doesn't care for me. What's next? I can't take this anymore. I'm going to jump; yup I'm going to jump. How do I get out of this damn bathroom without someone stopping me? I'll just figure it out when I get out there.

I opened the door and the nurse was standing there. She said, "I know it's hard for you right now, but you will be okay. You can try later; just save up your money for IVF or adopt." I wanted to slap the shit out of her.

I was just angry, not really at her, but at the whole situation. God just took my baby. This damn hospital, that doctor, and God just took my baby. No correction, my twins. My babies, they took my babies. I sobbed even more than before. Twins? Twins? How can that be? Why would God take both my babies and both my tubes? Why? In most cases, one gets through the tube and one gets stuck, but both babies? Both babies? *Lord, what did I do that was so bad that you took not one, but two babies and both my tubes? I can't take this pain; I want to jump or I'm going to drive myself crazy.*

I got back in the bed for a few more minutes while the nurse prepared my paperwork. My fiancée kept telling me that my family and friends were calling me. I didn't want to talk to anyone. Not one person. She just told me that everyone was thinking of me and praying for me. I didn't care; no one loved me, and no one cared about me. I wanted to jump.

I looked at my fiancée and said, "I just want to die right

Pushing Through

now. He said twins, right?"

She said, "Yes, babe, we will try again."

I wanted to slap the shit out of her too. Although I know she meant well and probably didn't know what to say, those just weren't the words I wanted to hear. I wanted to hear that we could still get pregnant the cheap, easy way; that we could try again and it wouldn't cost us $20,000.

They released me and I was wheeled to the car. My face had to be the most parched face in the world with my dried tears in streaks down it. We got in the car and I checked all my voicemail and text messages. I called my mom back and my son answered the phone. He asked why I was crying and what had happened to me. I told him that I had lost the baby that I had been pregnant with and was very distraught by it. All he heard was his mom on the phone crying really hard. He said he couldn't talk to me because I was making him cry.

So, my mom got on the phone and I explained everything to her. I told her, "I didn't tell anyone because of the way everyone responded to me when I said I wanted to try and have kids again."

She said, "You can't pay that any attention."

I said, "But I did, and although it hurt my feelings, I chose not to tell anyone about my pregnancy. The few people I did tell were very supportive about it."

My other line beeped and it was the fertility clinic, so I

Charise Marie

told my family I would call them back. The nurse from the clinic asked me what happened, so I told her the entire story. I told her how I came into the emergency room and they gave me the multiple ultrasounds; I told her about surgery and them finding that I had not one, but two babies in my tubes. I sobbed the entire time I was talking to her. I then told her that they took both of my tubes. She said she was sorry to hear it, that she would have the doctor contact me, and to get some rest.

During our entire ride home, my fiancée tried to soothe my pain by talking to me and trying to cheer me up with some music. I didn't want anything but my babies; that was it. She finally gave me the "Get Well Soon" balloon and a bag of my favorite candies to eat, but I had just eaten the yogurt the recovery room nurse gave me. I kept thinking of ways to die. I thought if I pulled the steering wheel while she's driving, then maybe we would fly into another car. If I pulled it to my side, I would die and she might just be injured. I didn't want to hurt her, just myself. The pain was so unbearable.

Soon, most of my family knew what had happened to me as I told my mom to tell them. I typed a really long message on social media and had hundreds of responses and private messages from so many women saying all kinds of great positive things.

I posted this on social media:

Hey FB. I'm having a hard time typing this but I was 6 weeks pregnant. Started experiencing severe pain early yesterday, talked to my doc she said go to ER but we went to the

Pushing Through

wedding festivities. They performed emergency surgery as they found out I was pregnant in 1 tube as he went in to remove the tube he saw I was pregnant in both tubes & had to remove both babies & both tubes. If it wasn't for my son I already have, my fiancée being by my side & the encouraging words I got from friends & FB, I'd jump off a building. Nobody knows what this shit feels like. I can't stop crying because.... just devastating. We left the hospital & DE & are on our way home. If I don't respond to any thing, please understand I'm not in the mood as I have also received negative comments.

I received so many comments and tons of messages after that posting. Some told me their stories by private message about how they lost their baby or their tubes. I was shocked by how many people said that they had similar experiences. Some chose to never have babies after that; some had children afterward. I was surprised by who these women were: They were women I talk to either in person or on social media daily. I quickly realized that there were a lot of women out there who just don't talk about this type of loss. They told me their entire stories and I no longer felt alone, but I was sad that this had happened to so many of us.

One lady suggested that I check out the therapy center where she worked. So, I told myself that Monday morning I would call to make an appointment.

A female relative texted me once I arrived home. She said some very encouraging words, but told me she was afraid to call me because I had just got out of surgery and was still in emotional pain. She said she would check on me the next day, and I said okay.

Charise Marie

My friends and more family members called and texted me as well. Most of them said they didn't want to bother me because I was resting and in pain. I just told them I would talk to them later. They said if I needed them, they were there for me. The only thing I wanted them to do was go to heaven and bring back my babies.

I kept crying even after I got home. I knew my fiancée hurt inside every time she looked at me and couldn't soothe my pain. She couldn't find a way to help me stop hurting so badly. I'm sure she was a little concerned after I expressed that I wanted to jump off a building and commit suicide. She kept asking me if I was okay, and I just kept telling her no, that I wanted my babies. She said we would try again, and I just looked at her because neither of us was sitting on $20,000.

I just wanted so badly to take the pain away from losing the babies, but I quickly thought that I couldn't be selfish and leave this world; I had a son already here who I had to finish raising. I'm very thankful that I have him. I guess the pain from the loss made me think I had no one. Although I have family and friends who love me, I felt no love that day. I just knew God had to hate me to have done this to me. No one knew what this pain was like. I felt so alone.

I woke up the next morning around 3:00 and Tiny was still asleep in bed. I went to the bathroom and told myself that yesterday was all a dream. "You're still dreaming," I said, but when I started to feel the pain in my stomach from the surgery, I knew it hadn't been a dream at all. All I could see was the doctor standing there, holding the pictures, saying I had lost a set of twins and my tubes. I just cried and

Pushing Through

cried. I wanted this nightmare to end, and to end fast.

I hopped on social media and began reading all the messages I had received from my social media friends. I cried so much that I think I could have filled up my bathtub. Later, I tried sliding back in bed as quietly as possible.

Once my fiancée Tiny and I woke up, she asked me how I was doing. I told her that I wanted this nightmare to be over. She just looked at me and said, "Babe, it's going to work out."

I said, "How? How will this work out?"

She said, "Pray on it."

I glared at her and said, "Pray on it; pray on it. You're out of your freaking mind. The God that I pray to daily knew I wanted to have another child for a very long time. I prayed and prayed and prayed some more that he would make me a mother again. I didn't pray for him to put me through this damn pain of getting pregnant and then losing the babies and my tubes. So, pray on it, is that what you say? You freaking pray on it. See what you get out of it. I've lost all my faith in God."

She said, "Do you think God or the doctors did this to you?"

I said, "Are you freaking kidding me? Am I not supposed to blame God for this? Seriously, answer me! Am I not supposed to blame him for taking not one, but two of my babies? Oh, and let's not forget that he took not one,

Charise Marie

but both of my tubes too. So yeah, my faith in him is gone. What a mighty God we serve, right? He's mighty alright. What do you know anyway? You never wanted to carry children. What do you really care? I carried those babies for six weeks. They weren't yours, they were mine. Did you really care anything about my babies? Did you?"

She got quiet. She knew not to say anything else because she knew that all my frustration was toward the pain I was feeling from the loss and not really toward her. I felt pretty bad later for taking things out on her, but I'm fairly sure she knew where my real anger was coming from and that I didn't mean all the things I said to her.

She saw me in physical pain and took my prescription to get filled at the pharmacy. As Tiny got outside she realized that her car was gone. She called me and said she needed to call the car dealership to see what happened. Once she got in from getting my prescription she called them and said she believe they came to get it because she was behind in payments. I didn't say anything because she was running around the house mad trying to figure out how she was going to get around without her car. We got into an argument because she said wow, you suffered a loss yesterday and I suffered one today. I swear I wanted to slap her silly. I was trying to figure out how losing her car was as bad as me losing my twins and my tubes. So of course, I snapped and cursed her out.

I jumped online to research some therapy centers that would treat me before I tried to commit suicide. I found some great groups on social media that were for women who had lost babies. I joined quite a few of them. Many women had lost babies through ectopic pregnancies like I had. There were also women who had suffered miscarriages, stillborn children, and even some who had delivered and had their babies die shortly after. It was just devastating. I found a group just for ectopic pregnancy victims and shared my story. The majority of the women who responded had never heard of being pregnant in both tubes and losing both.

Soon I started getting phone calls and messages from family and friends. My son even texted me daily messages, checking up on me in his own way.

"Hey Mom, what are you doing?"

I replied, "Lying here, resting."

He responded, "Okay."

I know my mom said that she explained it to him as best as she could, and even though he really didn't understand medically what happened, he knew his mom had lost a set of twins and was crying. It felt good to hear from him since he is a teenager. (Most times you only hear from them when they want money.)

A female relative texted me a sweet message and said that she didn't want to bother me. So, I called her. We talked, and the main thing that stuck in my head when she and I talked was the word "determined." She told me, "Have faith in God. He will help you get through this, and you will have kids someday soon."

Charise Marie

I said, "But I don't have thousands of dollars lying around; I spent nearly all my savings for this process."

She said, "One thing I've learned about you over the years is that you are very determined to get what you want, and you succeed each time. Girl, that's what I love about you. If you want something, you will get it. I know you will; I've seen it before."

I said, "Yeah, I hear you, but it will take me forever to come up with that kind of money. By then I will be in my fifties. It's not like $20,000 will drop in my lap tomorrow."

She said, "Yeah, but you never know how or when it will drop in your lap."

What she said about my determination has stuck with me since that day. She texted me scriptures or quotes every day and I truly appreciated it. It helped get me through some of the rough parts of each day.

But by the time Monday came, my fiancée was back at work and I was home alone. I woke up to an empty house and no babies in my belly. I cried and cried each moment of the day. I started to think about suicide again. I told myself that the pain was still unbearable, and I couldn't go on feeling this way every day for the rest of my life. I took the painkillers that were prescribed to me after my surgery. I took them with an over-the-counter painkiller as well. It was just a few extra pills than I normally take. I took almost a handful of them, thinking that it would take me out of my pain, out of this world, and away from what was going on.

Pushing Through

I felt very woozy when I woke up, and thought to myself that suicide attempt didn't work. Should I be glad that it didn't work? Should I be pissed off that it didn't? I didn't know how to feel right then, but the emotional pain to me was the worst.

I had heard over the years about how taking too many painkillers can kill you. That was my goal, but of course I didn't tell anyone that. I don't think anyone understood how badly I hurt inside over losing my babies. Why didn't suicide work for me? Why does God continuously want me to be in this pain? Why me? I really needed to know, why me?

My fiancée, family, and a few friends texted and called me and I answered back that I really didn't want to talk to anyone right then. Although I knew everyone meant well, I just couldn't deal with them and the pain. I worked hard to save up all that money and now, my babies, and my tubes were gone. I became extremely pissed off; even more so as I had not heard from the fertility clinic at all. I had just had an ectopic pregnancy where I lost my twins and tubes, and the doctor had not even called me to say anything.

When Tiny finally came home from work that night, she asked how I was feeling and how my day went. I told her that I had joined a few support groups on social media and called the therapy center. Unfortunately, I couldn't get an appointment right away. They had to match me with a therapist first. I said by then I would be lying in a pool of blood.

A few days went by and I became enraged. I still hadn't

Charise Marie

heard from my fertility doctor. I called her office and told her nurse that I was pissed off that she hadn't called to check on me. I said that she could have easily been greedy by getting me in there to try again with the $20,000 procedure. The nurse took my message and said she would have her call me. The doctor must've known how livid I was with her and that I meant business because she called me back in less than twelve minutes. She said that she wanted me to come in to discuss further options.

By now I no longer wanted to be under her care. I felt that she was in it for the money. In my eyes, she was cold and heartless. Here I was struggling to have something most women in this world could easily have, and she just threw me away. How could she not at least call me after such a devastating loss and say I'm sorry that you lost your babies?

I saw her the next day and she gave me the list of how much it would cost for me to try again. Her price for IVF was $27,000.

I listened to what she said as she tried to convince me to go back to work the next Monday. That was only a week out from surgery. She told me that I should be fine. I said that I wasn't fine; I was emotionally messed up over the loss. She finally gave me two more weeks out from work for a total of three weeks off.

A few days went by and it seemed like my tears would get tired of streaming down my face, but they didn't. I cried even more each day. I was cleaning up the kitchen one morning after I had breakfast and Tiny had left for work. As

Pushing Through

I was doing the dishes, I realized that I could easily make my family think that I accidentally cut myself on the sharpest knife I had in the soapy water. I needed to take this pain away and this might do the trick. Those stupid pills didn't seem to work, so let's try this. I then thought *No, don't use the knife to cut yourself. You will bleed out all over the floor and there will be blood everywhere. You don't want blood everywhere.* I then thought to myself, *What kind of crazy person thinks of killing themselves, then cares about the cleanup?* I knew I was certified crazy now.

While off from work, I saw a psychic reading studio outside of the city, and I looked at my fiancée and said, "I'm going in." She said that it wasn't of God, and I gave her the look of "it wasn't of God to take my babies." I think she felt the look I gave her. The psychic asked what I wanted to know, and I said, "Whatever you can tell me." She said that she could see that I was having some problems in my relationship. She looked at my hand and said I was meant to be a mother of four children. I chuckled. She then asked if I had lost a baby or had a miscarriage recently, and my mouth hit the floor. How could she have possibly known that I had just lost a baby? She said that she could also see that I would be having a nervous breakdown soon. I came out and told my fiancée what she had said, and she said, "See, why would she tell you that you are going to have a nervous breakdown? That is crazy. I told you they aren't real."

I said, "Well how did she know I had a miscarriage or lost a baby? How could she have known that?" My fiancée said it was because I was holding a pillow in my lap. I said "really," and we continued on walking.

Charise Marie

    I arrived back at work and my coworkers wanted to know why I was in the office and not home resting. I told them that my fertility doctor only gave me a few weeks off due to surgery. They told me that I needed another doctor to help me get together emotionally. I agreed, but there was nothing I could do about it.

    I was okay my first day back at work except for the people who knew my situation constantly checking on me. It was nice, but I didn't want to worry about my pain at work. I had just managed to stop crying every single day for three weeks straight, so I definitely didn't want to start crying at work.

    I researched a few infertility groups online to see which I could join in order to get support until I was able to connect with a therapist from the therapy place I had called. I joined one that ran the first Sunday of every month; it was a small one started by a woman who went through infertility herself. I felt pretty awkward because it was filled with women of different ethnicities and I was the only African-American woman there. Some of the women even had their husbands or boyfriends with them. I decided that I wanted to go to the first session by myself, so my fiancée had stayed home. It was an okay experience for my first time. I had a chance to tell my story, and everyone said "Wow!" when they heard me say I lost twins and both tubes. They said that they had never heard of that happening before. Most people have heard of women losing one baby and the other baby making it if pregnant with twins, or women losing a baby and a tube, but never both at the same time. I was now thinking about how odd my situation was.

Pushing Through

I looked up online losing two babies to ectopic pregnancies and found one woman in Australia who stated that she had lost her tubes and a set of twins at the same time.

I got home and told my fiancée how the session went. I then attended a later session with my fiancée the following month. I needed to find a way to keep myself sane and to keep myself from committing suicide.

I finally had a chance to get an appointment with my new therapist. We talked about my entire situation: how my partner and I started the whole baby journey, what it felt like when I found out I was finally pregnant, and how devastated I was when I lost them. It was just something I never would have imagined. I told her on a few different occasions how suicide was never talked about in my household growing up. All I heard was that it was a sin to commit suicide because you wouldn't go to heaven. As an adult, it wasn't talked about much either, but I would turn on the news or log on to a new site online and find that someone succeeded in committing suicide. I always wondered what made people want to take their lives. Were they crazy? What was so bad in life that would make someone want to take their own life? I found out the answer to that question the day my twins were taken from me. Most people never understand and will never understand the mind of someone who has committed or tried to commit suicide.

Charise Marie

March 2015

I went to therapy for months, every other Saturday to be exact. It was very helpful for me. I still experienced the hurt and pain, but I was able to find ways to cope with it. I threw myself into another business, hung out more with friends and family, and even tried to get back into reading books again.

The babies' due date was March 22nd, 2015. I decided to go to the store to get some latex balloons to release in honor of them had they been born that day. Since the ectopic pregnancy was so early on, and I didn't know what the sex of the babies was, I purchased three pink balloons and three blue balloons: two pinks in case they were girls, two blues in case they were boys, and one pink and one blue balloon in case they were a boy and a girl. My fiancée Tiny and I went to a local park and I cried hard but held it together. I said a prayer as I released each set of balloons. I told them how much I missed them and that for whatever unknown reason, God had needed them more than I did. It was devastating, but I had to come to terms with the loss with lots of prayer.

The weekend of my one-year anniversary loss of the twins I ran into some family members. I was told that a few of my relatives told my cousin that I was now jealous of her because she was pregnant. They told her to stay away from a girl like me because once we lose our babies we tend to be jealous and try to harm other people's babies. I was devastated when I found that out. Why would you tell her I would

Pushing Through

harm her baby just because I lost mine? I was hurt because we were all so very close and to turn her and other family members against me made me very upset.

When July 26th, 2015, rolled around, I cried my eyes out because it was one year after the ectopic tragedy had happened to me. One thing I would never have is an answer as to why it happened to me. I just continued to go to therapy and prayed a lot to keep myself from going crazy. Most people tell me that this is something I'm going to always reflect on because it's devastating to have to try so long to get pregnant and then lose not one, but two babies and both tubes at the same time in just ten days. God picked me to be their mother and experience this loss. I will never know why he picked me; maybe he felt as though I could handle this kind of loss.

My fiancée and I got up that morning and decided to visit this church we kept hearing about. I just couldn't sit in the house the entire day crying. We went to the church, and I don't know what happened, but it sounded like the pastor's sermon was speaking directly to me. Every time we bowed our heads in prayer, I couldn't help but cry and think of my loss. The sad thing was that I had lost all my faith in God when I lost the twins. I knew I had to find some kind of way to gain my faith back, and sure enough, that pastor made me believe again.

We met a few friends, Irene and Nic, after church and went to eat. I told my fiancée and friends that I could not sit in the house all day and cry, so they planned a day out. We ate at a restaurant and had a nice time laughing and being silly. Later, we went around to a department store and acted like fools, just having a fun time. We picked up a few items for the next stop: some games, snacks, drinks, and a small fold-up table. We then went to a park downtown and set up our chairs, table, and games. We chatted, laughed, played a few games, and ate our snacks. It was a good time.

I thanked everyone for staying out with me until late that night, and for keeping me laughing so I wouldn't be crying. We took pictures and went home. I thanked my fiancée Tiny again once we got home. I wanted her to know I appreciated the day.

September 2015

Most people kept telling me that I went back to work too early. They kept saying that I needed more time off to get myself together. I agreed, but my fertility doctor didn't see it that way. All she knew was that I had had surgery, and that three weeks was just enough time to recover. She clearly didn't think about my mental state. After the due date in March and one-year anniversary of the tragedy passed in July, I felt my blood pressure going up.

I went to my primary care doctor and she and the nurse told me I was way too young for a stroke. I was only thirty-six years old. They told me to please get rid of whatever it was that was bothering me. My blood pressure was extremely high, so it was time to take my medication again and relax.

I had an appointment with my therapist and she diagnosed me with Post Traumatic Stress Disorder (PTSD). She wrote me a note for three months leave from work to

Pushing Through

get any extra help I needed. My leave started the week of Thanksgiving. I finally had time to try and get more help. Unfortunately, since my job held my paycheck because the paperwork my therapist filled out multiple times wasn't to its liking, I could not afford to pay for the therapy sessions at my clinic. I pushed myself into all of my businesses more than ever this time around, and I also tried to pick up crocheting blankets and stuff. The crocheting didn't last too long. I never really learned how to do it the right way. I had watched many videos online for help, but whatever I was doing was not coming out the same way as they showed.

March 2016 rolled around and I decided to get a tattoo that read, "Twin Angels, 7-26-14 & 3-22-15" (the days on which I lost them and they would have been born). There is a pink and blue ribbon in the middle of it which represents the infancy loss ribbon. It is similar to when people get the cancer-related ribbons. I had this tattooed on March 22nd, 2016, as they would have turned one year old had they been born. I continued to see my therapist because their one-year birthday in March and the two-year anniversary of losing them in July were so close to each other. I wanted to make sure that I was sane and wouldn't try anything crazy.

For the first few years, every March and July were pretty hard for me. It was difficult to focus, to get out of bed, or even to do things around those times. I've been told that the pain will lessen as the years go on. I don't know how easy it will get, but I pray that one day I'll be able to say a prayer and a few words to them and smile knowing that for whatever God's reason was for taking them from me, it was a good reason. I may never understand his reason, but I've started telling myself that maybe they were sickly babies

Charise Marie

and he felt that with me being a sickly person, I wouldn't be able to handle them. Maybe he thought that I wasn't capable of handling twins. I just pray that I can come up with the money to have another child one day, so I can raise it and love it like a mother should.

Pushing Through

"Just because you loved and lost doesn't mean stop loving. If you have a nightmare, does it mean u stop dreaming?" – Jill Scott

Charise Marie
Chapter Eight: Dust Yourself Off and Try Again

April 2016

    I contacted a fertility clinic out of state that a few people in the social media group spoke highly of. They told me the rates were very reasonable; a lot of the women said that they had a great experience with it. Some had even gotten pregnant. It made me happy to hear about such great results. I did a lot of research on the clinic and then signed up as a patient. The clinic connected me with a travel coordinator because I was out of state. The travel coordinator had me set up an appointment with the doctor for an early Monday morning appointment in May. The doctor called me and asked me all kinds of questions regarding my infertility and the loss of the twins during my ectopic pregnancy. I told him that one baby was in each tube, and that they were unable to save either tube. He wasn't too shocked as he had heard of this thing happening before, but he said it was very rare. One to two percent to be exact.

    Over the next few weeks I spoke with the financial team, the travel team, and the nurses to help me achieve my ultimate goal: pregnancy. The staff at the clinic sent me all of the paperwork I needed to get started. The first thing to do was to call around in my hometown to find a clinic willing to do out-of-town monitoring and testing. I finally found a testing place where I was able to have my blood drawn. I

Pushing Through

had been searching around for another fertility clinic to do my monitoring and testing as I didn't want to return to the previous clinic I had used. I found a clinic and they told me that once my next cycle came that they would do my Hysterosalpingogram (HSG) and Sonohysterogram (SHG) tests.

When I spoke more with the nurse and she took further information from me, she said she didn't understand why my fertility doctor would request the HSG test as I no longer had my fallopian tubes. I told her that I had had that same test done before I became pregnant in 2014 and my tubes looked great. She suggested that I call my fertility clinic to see if we could bypass the HSG test. I spoke with my clinic and they agreed that I didn't have to have that test done as it would be a waste for me and would eventually cost money. Each test runs anywhere between six and eight hundred dollars. My fertility clinic sent me paperwork on which sperm banks to use, and my previous donor bank was not on the list. I was a little upset because now I had to search through thousands of new banks and donors. Even though my previous pregnancy resulted in an ectopic one, I did achieve pregnancy so we knew my donor's sperm worked. So, I started searching through the different sperm banks. There were very few African-American sperm donors from which to pick.

I started to think about whether it was my time to try again. Was I way out of my league when it came to putting out so much money that I barely had?

I had been speaking with another therapist, one my fiancée and I were seeing for our relationship issues. She was helping us with the loss of my fiancée's mother, the loss of

Charise Marie

my twins, and other things that came about in our relationship that were making us not be nice to one another. We constantly argued and really needed a therapist to step in and help us out.

One evening she spoke about the fact that my fiancée's anger over the loss of her mother and my anger over the loss of my twins was coming out toward one another. She gave us plenty of strategies to try. She suggested that I go to the local hospital and volunteer for the "Hug an Infant" program. I told her that I didn't think it would be a good idea because I wouldn't be able to take them home. That process would hurt me even more. I want to take a baby home with me for good. I said if she knew of a program where I could take an infant home then I would be willing, but I didn't want to go hold and hug a baby and leave. I didn't think I could handle that just yet. She then told us that her granddaughter had a doll that looked very real. She told us that the doll was pretty expensive because the person who makes the doll makes it custom to what you want as far as looks, complexion, etc. Some dolls even make a little noise. They are life-like dolls.

I went home and my fiancée Tiny and I researched these dolls. I immediately thought that I had started to lose my mind looking at the dolls. I became fascinated with them. I was about to purchase one, but did more research and found that there were tons of people who designed them, some better than others. The dolls ranged from four hundred to seven hundred and fifty dollars. I even found a few dolls that were much higher. I was willing to pay the $750 for the one doll I saw. I told my fiancée that I wanted to get one and start purchasing clothes and diapers from the local

Pushing Through

department store. I just wanted to have a baby in my arms and I was willing to try this doll.

I slept on the idea and woke up the next day with the dolls still on my mind. So, I did more research on them. I then thought that I was losing my mind.

How would this doll replace the loss of my twins?

I felt that having this doll might make me crazier than I was when I wanted to commit suicide. I texted a few friends and told them about the dolls. I sent them pictures and videos of these dolls as well. They told me that I had lost my mind and I laughed but told them that our therapist suggested it. They didn't like the idea and said the same thing my fiancée did: that I should speak to my regular therapist.

That weekend I spoke with my regular therapist and she and I played out the pros and cons of having one of the dolls. We both came to the decision that it wasn't in my best interest to get one. She felt that it would set me back to feeling the hurt and pain of the loss. Looking at, caring for, and holding the doll would keep me in a place that might not have me continue on with the IVF process. She felt as though it would make me scared of moving forward, and that I would become lost holding a doll. This doll is not a real person, but I would be caring for it as if it were. Buying clothes and diapers for it and taking it out in a stroller would make me crazier. I agreed with her, but the doll was still in the back of my mind for a while.

I later let the idea go. I started thinking about all the money I could save toward having the IVF process instead.

Charise Marie

Although we knew how expensive IVF is, if I kept saving and saving, I should be able to do it.

July 2016

    I finally had the SHG test done on my uterus and the doctor told me that it looked great. There were no fibroids, and the lining of my uterus looked good too. After stressing over that for weeks, I was relieved that it was some good news. Now I just had to get the medications I needed. I had done a lot of research on the medications that I believed I would use. I was told by many of the women in the groups that the medications could run up to five thousand dollars each. I was really scared that that would be the case for me, and that I wouldn't have enough money to purchase the medications and have the IVF done too. I used nearly all my savings for the IUIs I had done back in 2014. I did have bills and a life to live, so for me to save up another $10,000 for this procedure was freaking me out. I spoke with the staff at the fertility clinic and they had most of the paperwork they needed, so now they needed me to purchase the medication. The nurse sent the list of medications to a pharmacy and the price was $3040.40. My mouth hit the floor when the pharmacist started forming the words "three thousand." I immediately told him thank you and that I would have to contact another pharmacy because that was way too much money. I found another pharmacy and the pharmacist told me that some of the medications were not covered under their half-off medication programs. I applied anyway and got fifty percent off one of the medications. My insurance rejected the rest because they were not known as a

Pushing Through

mail-order pharmacy.

 I contacted my clinic and had them send the prescription to yet another pharmacy. I told my fiancée that I would not stop until I had all the medications at a very low price. Another pharmacy contacted me and said they had my medication list and that they could get all the medications, except for two, for $420. One of the medications that was not available through them was ordered from my local pharmacy. When I initially called, the pharmacist told me the price for the one medication was $167. Although I was very upset, I told her to order it. But when I called the pharmacy to tell them that I had received the phone call stating my prescription for the medication had been filled, she told me the cost was $30. I ran into the pharmacy really quickly and grabbed it. I was ecstatic. Now, as I was waiting to hear about the last medication, another pharmacy told me the price was $474. I was livid. They told me that price was with the fifty percent discount. I thanked them and told them that I would not be purchasing the medication from them.

 I called my clinic and told them to find another medication that did the same thing but was cheaper. They said they had another one and would call it in to my other pharmacy. Once I contacted that pharmacy, they told me that with my fifty percent discount, the price for all six medications was $350. Although that price was still very high to me, I decided to pay the $350 because it didn't seem like I would get this medication any cheaper than that.

Charise Marie

September 2016

The next step was waiting until my menstrual cycle started. I felt premenstrual symptoms while I was in Atlanta, Georgia, for my travel business convention, I became an independent travel agent in January. Back in my hotel room that Friday night, I did the bring-it-on-menstrual-cycle dance: I danced around the hotel room saying, "Come on cycle, come on."

Sure enough, my menstrual cycle began on Saturday morning, so I called the clinic bright and early Monday morning. They told me to set up an appointment for my ultrasound and blood work. The clinic called me later that day after my appointment and told me that the results were okay but not great; I had cysts on my ovaries. I was devastated. I wanted to give up, but the nurse said not to worry. The doctor had said that all I needed to do was take birth control pills and that should shrink the cysts. They would send me in for another ultrasound and more blood work after I took the pills for two weeks.

The end of September came and I was now done with the birth control. I went to my appointment and got the results I wanted: the cysts were gone. Thank God! The doctor told me to start certain medications for the next few days and then they would let me know what to do next. They also wanted me to have my blood drawn and have an ultrasound every Monday, Wednesday and Friday. I did this for a week.

Pushing Through

October 2016

 I needed a refill on my medications by October because the five to six days' worth of medications I had were running out. I called the pharmacy I ordered them from and they told me that the medicines were not covered by my insurance policy and that the previous co-pay was not available. I asked what this meant and he told me that I had to pay $3066. I was like, "You must be kidding me." I called the clinic and told them, and they got in touch with my insurance company. I already knew that fertility medications were not covered under my job insurance, but somehow, I had gotten $3,000 worth of medications for $450 the previous month. The lady at the clinic called me and told me that my insurance had made a mistake before because it hadn't realized that the medications were for IVF. Now they were refusing to give me the medications. I would have to pay the out-of-pocket cost for them. I called around to multiple pharmacies in Pennsylvania and New York and most said they would cost anywhere between $2250 and $6000. I was freaking out. I still had to pay for the IVF procedure. How was I going to afford these medications? I jumped on social media and asked my fertility/baby groups whether anyone knew of any cheaper pharmacies and was told of one not too far away. I called them and they told me it would be two thousand dollars for the medications. I told them that I would call them back once I spoke to my clinic.

 I finally heard from my clinic and they told me that my ovaries seemed to be moving very slowly with my current medications, and that I should up the dosage. I was torn the entire day because now all I wanted to do was give up. I didn't have it in me to keep hearing bad news. I wanted

Charise Marie

to give up so badly. My fiancée Tiny asked me why, and I said that I couldn't take the pain anymore. I placed a post on social media that said I was heartbroken, and that God was not answering my prayers. Everyone told me that God would answer in his time. I've always hated when people say that, but they were right.

I got up the next morning, and while I was in the shower getting ready for work, all I did was cry and pray, pray and cry. I did my normal morning prayer and then I said, "God, I know everything is in your time, but I have exhausted nearly all of my money. Now needs to be the time, God. I'm begging and pleading with you. Please help me make the right decision today about getting the medicines and moving forward. God, I need a sign telling me to move on. I have faith this will work, but I need an extra sign from you; some kind of guarantee or something, God, please. I don't think I can take this; I'm not as strong as you think."

I got a call later on from the nurse at the fertility clinic who gave me instructions as to what I needed to do next. I had to up my dosages on my medications and add another one. I thanked her and we hung up.

I called about an hour later and asked the nurse questions that had started bothering me. I said, "I know you are not God and cannot give me a definite or guaranteed answer."

She said, "I can't, but I will try my best to answer you."

I said, "If I up my dosage and add this medication, is it possible that my eggs will grow to the size you want in or-

Pushing Through

der to move forward with IVF, or should I just wait and try again next month?"

She said, "Yes, there is a strong possibility they will grow."

I said, "I don't have three thousand dollars now, and I won't next month or the next. I need to know whether I have a chance now." She said that I had a chance, and I said, "That's all I needed to hear for me to move forward."

I called the pharmacy and placed the order refill for two thousand dollars. I prayed as I called them: God, I don't have any more money. I have nearly depleted everything I have, so I need this to happen for me this time. Please, God, please. I know things are done in your time, God, but I need this now more than ever. Financially, this is my last chance. God, I'm begging you.

I told the pharmacy that I would be there closer to closing time. I was on the bus on my way to pick up the medications and it would take me over an hour to get out there. I asked them to please stay open until I arrived.

Financially, this was extra draining and extra hard on me, especially since my fiancée could never help me with any of the costs of these procedures. She always said that she just didn't have thousands of dollars lying around. So, I did everything on my own once again.

I got off the bus and made it to the pharmacy just in time. They asked me how I had found out about them, and I told them "social media" and the owner laughed. He then

Charise Marie

asked me how I found out about the fertility clinic in another state, and I told him, "social media." I said, "See how useful social media really is?"

He laughed and said, "Yes. I'm hoping we can get on your fertility clinic's list to present medications to their patients, so I thank you so much for coming here. Most of our patients are from around here and the surrounding areas."

I got home later that evening and had to do an adult-toy party. I did my injections as soon as I got back home. I started to feel a little bit better once I prayed and put all my faith in this procedure.

I went to my regular appointments the next week for blood work and ultrasound. By Thursday, the doctor told me that everything looked great and that they wanted to do the retrieval on Saturday. I was so happy to hear that and was extremely excited that I had made the decision to keep going.

My fiancée Tiny and I arrived late Friday night. They did my egg retrieval at 7:30 Saturday morning and told me that they were able to retrieve five eggs. It didn't sound like a lot compared to some of the women on social media who had had fifteen to thirty eggs retrieved. The good thing was that I was still optimistic as one lady pointed out that it was about quality not quantity. All I needed was one good egg, just one. It was pretty evident because in another post I saw, the woman said that she had twenty-seven eggs retrieved and only ten or so fertilized. The rest they froze.

We left midday Sunday, and as we were on the bus going

Pushing Through

home, the nurse called me and told me that out of the five they got from me, three were doing extremely well. They planned on doing the transfer on Tuesday.

I decided to take vacation from work from Tuesday to Thursday because they had already told me that if they retrieved my eggs on Saturday then I would most likely have the transfer on Tuesday. It would be a day-three transfer. I booked my bus ticket for late Monday into midday Wednesday and printed out the tickets once we got off the bus.

I got a phone call that scared the life out of me on the Monday before my transfer. The nurse said that she didn't think it would be good to do a day-five transfer because the eggs probably wouldn't make it. I started getting hysterical. I said, "What do you mean? I spoke with someone yesterday and they told me that I had five eggs retrieved and three are doing extremely well. I'm already set to arrive tonight for a day-three transfer tomorrow."

She said, "Oh, you are?"

I said, "Yes."

She then told me that she needed to check the records because she had overlooked what the other nurse had written. She said that she was glad that I told her because she had wanted to suggest Tuesday which was better. The eggs may not have made it to day five. So, I booked the same hotel for Monday night to Wednesday afternoon.

The hotel was accommodating; I told them that I was having a procedure and they gave me a handicap-accessi-

Charise Marie

ble room. Before I left home, the clinic asked me whether I wanted to do an acupuncture treatment. I immediately said no. The nurse laughed and asked if I knew much about it and I didn't. She then explained it and made an appointment for 7:45 a.m.

I arrived Tuesday morning and found out that I had to pay for the acupuncture; I had assumed it was part of the package, but I still went along with it. She did a full explanation and then took me to the women's locker room so I could change into a robe and slippers and lock up my clothing and valuables. I went into the waiting area where the technician called for me. My pre-transfer acupuncture took about forty-five minutes. She then took me downstairs to have my transfer done. It was beautiful.

I had a chance to meet the doctor again and ask last-minute questions. I decided, along with the doctor, that it would be best to place two eggs in me and freeze the last one for a later time. They then told me every single step he and the nurse were doing as they did it: the insertion of the speculum and the catheter, and then the ultrasound to see where to place the embryos in my uterus. Luckily, I didn't feel much and everything went very well.

The acupuncturist came back to get me for my post-transfer session and it lasted approximately thirty minutes. They released me and I went back to my room. I was told to receive regular blood work six days later and to stay on all the injections I was currently taking. I was to continue doing the injections in my bottom and inserting the medications into my vaginal area.

Pushing Through

My next appointment would be on Halloween, a week later, but I was to wait thirteen days after my transfer to have my last blood test. I hoped that the blood drawn would determine that I was pregnant. Now I was just in the two-week waiting period. They told me to resume all activities but not to participate in anything strenuous, or to drink caffeinated beverages or eat many greasy foods. I was just waiting for the results. The two-week waiting period for beta results was torture. All I wanted to do was take the test and scream. The doctor told me that I couldn't experience stress, so all I thought were happy, positive thoughts that bring happy, positive results.

I did blood work six days after my transfer. I got a phone call from the fertility clinic stating my thyroid levels were pretty high. My thyroid-stimulating hormone (TSH) levels had gone from 1.27 on October 15th, which was the day of my retrieval, to 1.94 on October 18th, the day of my transfer, to 4.2 on October 24th. She explained that the TSH level should be just less than three. I was certainly praying that nothing had harmed the two embryos. All I asked for was healthy babies; that was all I wanted and prayed for. I would be okay if even one embryo didn't take. I just wanted at least one to be healthy. That was all I cared about.

Charise Marie

Monday, October 31st

The day finally came for me to go to the clinic to have my blood drawn for my beta results. I normally got to the monitoring clinic around 7:15 a.m. for my 7:30 or 8:00 appointment for either blood work or blood and ultrasound.

I would usually get a call from the clinic early afternoon with my results. This day, however, she called me at 9:55 a.m., which was unusual for them so I got scared. I still tried to remain as positive as possible. The nurse said, "They processed your blood work very fast."

I said, "Oh wow, they did it already?"

"You are pregnant!"

I said, "Thank you, Jesus!"

She said, "Your beta levels are 254 and we need you to come back in two days for another set of beta results."

I cried until I couldn't cry any more. Did she say I was pregnant? Dear God, all I ask is that you protect the body that these two embryos were placed in, and please, God, keep them healthy.

I couldn't call Tiny because she was at work, so I texted her: CALL ME RIGHT AWAY! She called shortly after and I

Pushing Through

cried on the phone and said, "I am pregnant! Can you believe it?"

She said, "Really?"

I said, "Yes!"

A few close friends who knew I was having the procedure had been asking how things were going the entire time since I received the procedure up until I had to wait for today's results. So, I texted them and told them the good news. They were ecstatic for me, of course, since they certainly knew my whole story.

I went into the clinic a few days later to have my blood drawn for the next set of results. The beta levels should be doubling every few days. My second set of beta results was 853. I was thrilled! This was great news because my numbers had tripled. The nurse at the fertility clinic told me to schedule my ultrasound to see the sacs, heartbeats, and viability. I scheduled that for the next week.

I went to the appointment for my blood work and ultrasound and was extremely nervous. Did both babies make it? Will I be sad if one didn't make it? Should I be happy that one made it and sad that the other one didn't make it? What if one split and it's triplets? All the what-ifs ran through my mind. I just prayed that everything would be alright. The nurse told me to drink thirty-two ounces of water to make sure my bladder was full for the ultrasound. She did the abdominal ultrasound and she said she couldn't see anything. I was immediately scared because I thought back to when I had had my ectopic pregnancy and she told

Charise Marie

me she couldn't find anything. The nurse then said, "Let me try the transvaginal ultrasound since it is still early in the pregnancy." I started praying, God, please not again. God, please not again. I'm telling you that I won't be able to handle that again. She was able to find one gestational sac during the transvaginal ultrasound. I let out a huge sigh of relief. She asked me how many eggs I had transferred and I told her.

She said, "Right now, I just see one."

I put my clothes on while thinking about how sad I was that she only saw one. I had had my hopes set on both showing. I texted my fiancée and she immediately called me. I told her that I was having a bittersweet moment. She said, "Don't focus on two; as long as we have one healthy him or her that's all that matters."

I told her, "Yes, I'm happy that she did see something, but I can't help but feel sad that the other one is not showing up."

It's hard knowing that you had two placed but only one shows up. I felt like crying on the bus ride home. I thought to myself, I guess two is better than one, but one is always better than none. I had to look at it that way. I talked to the ladies in the groups I'm in on social media and they all said, "Don't panic. Five weeks is really early to see anything. Give it another one to two weeks and you should hear something."

My fertility clinic called to tell me that everything looked good, and that the ultrasound showed a viable

Pushing Through

pregnancy. My third beta results were 11,642, and my thyroid levels had gone down significantly. I was so happy to hear that. The nurse then told me to schedule my next ultrasound. After that, they would be able to release me from their care as I would graduate to maternity care or a labor and delivery specialist. I called the walk-in clinic and scheduled my ultrasound for the day after Thanksgiving at 7:30 a.m. Sitting around and waiting those next few weeks made me lose a lot of patience (and I already had none).

In the meantime, I'd been experiencing a lot of nausea each day. I never had any morning sickness or nausea with my son, but now I was nauseated every day. I didn't know if it's the medicine I was taking or if I was just sick because of the baby. I also noticed that I had heartburn every day. I didn't want to have to down a whole bottle of heartburn pills daily. I had only had heartburn closer to the end of my first pregnancy. Most people at that time told me that he would have a head full of hair since I was experiencing heartburn so badly. He did have a head full of hair when he was born, but I thought it's too early to tell with this baby. I told my fiancée, "I think this baby might be a girl because of all the things I'm experiencing. I know they say every baby is different, but this baby is a girl. But as long as he or she is healthy, that is all that matters to me."

The nurse told me at the next ultrasound that she was able to see the baby, and the heartbeat was 170. It was great news to hear. She printed out a picture of the ultrasound and it looked weird. I was told that the circle over top of the baby was a yolk sac. I had placed two embryos in me so I was hoping that it was two babies, but so far they keep telling me that it was only one baby. I was disappointed, but

Charise Marie

I quickly realized that no matter what, I was still lucky and blessed to be able to have at least one.

My appointment with the obstetrician-gynecologist (OB-GYN) was scheduled for the beginning of December. My fertility clinic released me from their care and took me off all of my medication. They congratulated me and sent me on my merry old way.

I had a chance to meet the new OB-GYN and she seemed okay but didn't really seem too personable. She didn't give me any advice or ask if I had any questions about anything. I don't know if it was routine for her to just do a Pap smear, an ultrasound, and to discuss my medical background, but I wasn't feeling her. They scheduled me for the last day of December and told me that the doctor I had just seen would not be in that week. The receptionist asked if I wanted to see another doctor, and I told her, "Yes, a female doctor."

I had been really sick for a few weeks; I was very nauseated and had lots of gagging. I've never been one to vomit when ill, but with this baby I had my first vomit session. I was very shocked one day when I kept gagging, and something said run to the bathroom; this is the big one. When I actually vomited this time around I knew I had to have a little proof so I took a picture of it. I had had a lot of heartburn as well which I thought was pretty weird for being so early on in the pregnancy. I did have a chance to read a few articles on heartburn in the early weeks that I found on the baby sites. I was pretty shocked that it was so common in the beginning. I had only heard of heartburn occurring toward the end of pregnancies, which usually meant that the baby had a lot of hair. The first thing I thought was Sheesh,

Pushing Through

does this baby have hair already? My cravings had also been pretty funny since becoming pregnant. My fiancée Tiny laughed at me each time I craved something different. Some weekends I would get up around 4:00 a.m. craving pineapples. There had been a few times that I'd craved pickles, crab legs, burritos and ice cream. Most of the time, if I smelled it or saw it, I wanted it.

On Christmas Day, I surprised my family by telling them that I was pregnant. I gave my son a little box that I decorated with the words "Big Brother?" My parents' box said "Grandparents Again?" The inside of the boxes said "July 2017" and contained copied pictures of the first ultrasound I had taken a few weeks ago. My mom immediately knew what the ultrasound was, but we had to explain it to my son. Then I opened up my sweater and on my shirt was a picture of a baby peeking out of a hole. It read, "Hiding Until July 2017."

Everyone seemed to be very happy. My son asked how long I had known, and I told him since Halloween. I think he was a little upset because he asked me why I hadn't told him. I explained to him that people usually wait until after three months to announce pregnancies. By that time you are known to have a viable pregnancy. My mom and cousin helped me explain it to him a little more. I told them that I didn't know the gender of the baby yet, but that I took the genetic test the previous week. That test would tell me the sex of the baby and whether it had Down syndrome. My son was very excited, and he was adamant that he didn't care what the sex of the baby was, that he or she would be very protected no matter what. I was excited to hear that. I know he wanted a baby brother or sister growing up, but I hadn't been too sure about how he would feel about having one now that he was older.

Pushing Through

"Be strong. Things will get better. It might be stormy now but the rain won't last forever." – Unknown

Charise Marie
Chapter Nine: Unexpected

My birthday is in the beginning of January so a few friends; Heaven, Kelly, Denise and I went away to Maryland for some food, fun, and relaxation without our mates. The four of us drove in one car and had a nice time just laughing and singing to the music. Once we arrived, we checked in at the hotel and then decided to head to the mall area to do some light shopping and grab some dinner. I received a phone call from my OB-GYN's office just as we were leaving. They had the results of my test. She asked what news I wanted to hear first, and I told her that I only cared about the health of the baby. She told me that the baby didn't have Down syndrome or any of the other syndromes tested. I said, "Thank God," as I was happy about that.

She said, "As far as gender goes, what do you and your spouse want?"

I said, "My fiancée wants a girl and I just want a healthy baby, but if I have to choose, I would say a boy. I don't know how to braid hair or know anything about all the pink girly stuff." She laughed.

She said, "Well congratulations, your fiancée wins; it's a girl."

I laughed and said, "Oh wow!" as a tear came to my eye. I'd be happy regardless of what I was having, as long as the baby was healthy.

Pushing Through

My friends wanted to know if everything was okay. I said, "Yes. The doctor called to tell me that the baby has none of the tested syndromes and to tell me the gender." So of course, they all wanted to know what it was. I told them that they had to wait a month until the gender-reveal party. I laughed but I don't think they liked my laughter.

We left and went to the nearby mall for some food and shopping. We had a nice time and picked some great food to eat. We then walked around the whole mall and checked out the great shops. We had to do a little shopping while there, of course. I picked up some great perfumes and pocketbooks. We sat around and joked and laughed at the things we saw. I got a little woozy from all the walking, so two of my friends, Kelly and Denise, went into a store and my best friend Heaven and I sat on a bench so I could rest for a second. We sat there and chatted for a bit, and when our other friends came out of the store, we were all ready to go back to our room.

We decided to play some games after we put away our newly bought items. We played one of the apps on my phone. I coughed as we were laughing and being silly trying to guess what one of the answers was, and I immediately felt a gush. I thought, Wow did I just tinkle on myself? So, I ran into the bathroom where I saw a ton of blood in my underwear and down my leg. Then I felt two large blood clots come out and I immediately got very worried and started saying a ton of prayers. God, please, I'm begging you, do not let these two things that just dropped out of me be my baby. God, I can't do this. And this is my birthday weekend also. I don't want to remember my birthday weekend as having lost another baby. God, come on and work with me

Charise Marie

here, work with me.

I wiped myself off then jumped up and opened the door and told my friends, "I think I just miscarried those babies." They all ran into the bathroom and saw the blood on the floor and all over the toilet. I kept saying "I just lost my baby, I just lost my baby." I told them to dig out whatever was in the toilet, and my one girlfriend said, "That's the tissue you used to wipe with."

I said, "No, that thing under it is a huge clot. That's my baby."

They took me out of the bathroom and dug out the clot with the towels and cups in the room. I started praying to God again. I kept saying, "God, please do not let this be my baby, please, please, please. I can't take another loss, God. I swear, I can't. Please let that be the baby they couldn't find and not the baby in the ultrasound." My best friend Heaven came out of the bathroom praying. She then grabbed me and I asked her, "Was that my baby?"

She looked at me and said, "You know I would never lie to you. It does appear to be a large clot that could be a baby."

I told them to open the door as I felt a large gush coming down my leg; more blood was coming out. I asked them, "Did you see if that was my baby? I'm three months pregnant and that clot felt like the size they say the baby would be now. Was that my baby? Please don't lie to me guys, was that my baby?"

Pushing Through

The other two said, "We would never lie to you. It appears to be a baby to us."

I started feeling very faint and asked one to grab my phone so I could call my fiancée Tiny to let her know what had happened. As I was on the phone telling her, my best friend offered to clean me up in the shower, but I said no. My friends helped clean up the blood on the bathroom floor, tub, and toilet.

My fiancée was shocked, and I told her to pray that the baby was still there. She asked whether I was going to go to the hospital, and I said, "I'll see if I continue to bleed. It might have been the baby they said they couldn't find. I'm just going to pray." We prayed together on the phone. It didn't help ease my mind very much.

We went to bed and by morning I just had light spotting. I kept praying and praying. I continued on with my birthday weekend, trying to be happy and not think of the possible loss of yet another baby.

We got on the road on Sunday and Tiny said that she would pick me up. She and my best friend both decided that they were going to go to the hospital with me to see if the baby was still there. I burst into tears on the way to the hospital. "I don't understand what God is doing to me. Does he not want me to be a mother again? Am I a bad mother, is that why he took my twins and won't allow me to have another baby? Why me, God, why me?" My best friend Heaven rubbed my back, said a prayer, and told me she loved me.

We arrived at the hospital and they asked questions and

Charise Marie

drew blood. I was in my room waiting for the ultrasound technician to arrive. They said they weren't a hospital equipped with baby machines, so they had to call someone in. The ultrasound technician finally arrived. I prayed multiple times on my way down the hallway to the back: God, please do not let that have been my baby. I closed my eyes really tightly as I got up on the hospital bed and said another two or three prayers. The technician asked what brought me in and I told her the story. She started doing the ultrasound and told me that my baby was right there. I wanted to see it so she turned the screen around and there was my baby! I was shocked because most technicians in the hospitals won't tell you any results; you have to wait for the doctor. I think she felt sorry about my situation and really wanted to tell me because she knew how important it was to me and how anxious I was feeling. I just kept saying "Thank You, Jesus! Thank You!" I arrived back into my room and told Tiny and Heaven that the baby was still there. We were all elated! I cried happy tears but still was wondering whether the clot had been the second embryo.

I went in for an emergency appointment with my OB-GYN and told her the story. She took the blood clot and said that she would test it. I told her that we kept it on ice the whole time. She examined me and said that the baby's heart rate was great and not to worry about anything. She did say, though, that because of my history with the loss of my twins and now this situation that she felt that I needed to be out of work for the duration of the pregnancy. She didn't want any more incidents to happen because the next time it might not turn out so good. So, she put me on medical leave from work. I told my job and submitted my medical claim with the insurance company.

Pushing Through

I planned a small gender-reveal party with friends. I rented a room at one of the popular restaurants in town and ordered some appetizers for everyone attending. I purchased some team-boy and team-girl stickers, a few pink and blue decorations, and, of course, the bag with the balloons in it for the reveal. I asked everyone to pick out a boy name and a girl name from the six we had chosen and written on the board. So, I had to find a way to trick my friends because most know me as just being silly. I wanted a healthy baby and my fiancée wanted a girl. Either way, I was happy to be having a baby. I had put blue and pink balloons in the bag. I went to the bag and everyone started screaming, "Team boy! Team girl!" I put my hand in the bag and pulled out a blue balloon. Those who said "team boy" were happy. I then said, "Sike!" and pulled out all the pink balloons and everyone went crazy. I shed a few tears because it meant so much to me that everyone shared that moment with Tiny and I.

I went in for my routine OB-GYN appointment. The nurse weighed me and took my urine sample as usual. She then came in the room to take my blood pressure. She said that my blood pressure was a bit high: it was 160/90. I said, "Wow, that is pretty high." She said she would let the doctor know before she came in to see me. I took a few full-body pictures to show off my belly and how much it had grown in six months as I waited for the doctor. I hadn't gained a lot of weight so far in this pregnancy, though. My doctor finally came in and said, "What is going on, girl?" She checked my pressure again and this time it was 162/105. She called down to the hospital and told them I was coming in to be monitored. She said it could be preeclampsia.

Charise Marie

I ended up being there for two hours. The baby was not cooperating with the heart-rate monitor, so they did an ultrasound and she was fine. My pressure finally went down to 115/52, which was low enough for them to release me. My fiancée came to pick me up from the hospital and asked how the baby was doing. By this time, we had already given the baby a name: Baby Firecracker. She was sure living up to her name!

My job contacted me to ask if I had heard anything about the medical insurance claim. I had not. I called the insurance company and was told that they had denied my claim. I would not be receiving any FMLA benefits while I was out on leave. I was very upset because now I would have no means to take care of bills, myself, or even the baby. I asked them if there was a reason the doctor at the insurance company denied my claim. The agent told me that he believed it was because I hadn't bled more than one day. I was floored. Had they wanted me to keep bleeding until I lost my baby? It was stated on the paperwork that I had a threatened miscarriage and my doctor wanted me out on leave, but the claim was still denied. I was so upset. I went into a depression because that would have been my biggest source of income. Now what was I to do? My son's prom was coming up, his graduation, the baby shower, the baby, and a host of other things as well. My fiancée and mom said that they would help me as much as possible. My mom was on disability so I knew I would have to try hard not to rely on her because she needed all her money for her home. It was going to be a tough road not having any money coming in and having to rely on others.

It was really tight for months. Every penny was

Pushing Through

squeezed left and right, but the bills kept piling up. My fiancée helped me pay my internet and appliance rental bill one month. I kept asking myself how I was going to be able to take care of the baby. I realized, though, that I would never regret my decision. No matter what, God had a plan. I just didn't know what it was. I just wish I knew what his plan was.

Every morning I tried my hardest to get out of bed. I didn't want to talk to anyone but my mom and my fiancée, and half the time I didn't want to talk to them. I didn't talk to family, friends, coworkers, anyone. Some of my friends thought I was neglecting them by not contacting them. I felt that they were selfish because they could contact me if they cared anything about me: Friendship is a two-way street. I was sinking into a depression. I constantly blamed myself for everything that happened to me. I didn't want to feel like I was to blame, and I certainly didn't want to blame the baby.

For days I got up and just started crying out of nowhere. I dragged myself around the house. My fiancée Tiny didn't pay attention to the way I was feeling. I guess she just thought it was either due to the pregnancy or me just being me. Most days I felt like I was going to faint. I'm not sure if that was a result of losing all that blood in January, but the feeling was not nice. I had a few friends who would contact me via text message, and I appreciated them. They checked in on me to see how the baby and I were doing. The messages made my day sometimes but being depressed still made the days hard.

My mom gave my son some money to get his tuxedo

Charise Marie

for prom and said she would pay for the rest of it, but my fiancée Tiny paid off the rest of it instead. My parents gave me money for his prom pictures, and my fiancée took him to the prom in her car. I felt so badly that I couldn't provide more for him, but he completely understood and isn't the kind of kid who wanted all the hoopla anyway.

    My son's prom and the baby shower were on Memorial Day weekend. We had to cut back a lot on what I wanted for the baby shower. My fiancée paid for everything upfront, and I planned on giving her my half of what was spent once I came into some money like we discussed. Luckily, I had relatives who helped me with the cake and food with their food stamps. My fiancée paid the coordinator to decorate and the chef at her job to prepare the food. She also did other little odds and ends, and I had a few dollars to help with the drinks. My son escorted me into the baby shower and it was beautiful to see all of our friends, family, and church family there. I looked around at how beautiful it all looked and was a little teary about everything. I was surprised by how many gifts the baby had received when they pulled them around in front of me. The next day we had a few more friends (who had been unable to make it to the shower) come to our home to drop off gifts for the baby. Once everyone left, I looked at Tiny and broke down and cried. She asked why I was crying, and I said, "God is good." I cried because I had been struggling for the last few months trying to figure out how this baby would have all the things she needed, and in the blink of an eye she had everything she needed from all our wonderful friends and family. It was a beautiful feeling knowing that God had heard my prayers.

Pushing Through

I felt super bad because my son had his college papers coming in the mail and he was accepted to a local college. I was super excited but felt so horrible inside. They needed me to pay a $300 admissions fee for him and he would be able to start the summer program. I was devastated. I called my mom and told her and she said she would try to see who she can borrow the money from. I told her don't worry I will see what I can do when I speak with admissions. Once I spoke with admissions they told me to fill out his financial aid online and I did. I even sent in all the necessary paperwork. Unfortunately, he wasn't able to be enrolled for the summer or fall semester. I was so hurt that I couldn't provide for my child to do the one thing he wanted so badly to do and that's go to college.

At thirty-three weeks, I started going to my doctor appointments twice a week. They wanted me to get a stress test done twice a week and an ultrasound once a week. They weren't able to get the baby's heart rate at times, so I would be in there a little bit longer than normal. The doctors always told me to make sure I felt at least ten movements every two hours.

One day I didn't feel her move for almost six hours. I got worried. We went down to the hospital around 7:00 that evening, and they had a bit of a hard time finding her heart rate on the stress monitor. She finally woke up and moved around for about forty-five minutes. They decided to give me an ultrasound while I was there to check her movements and heart rate on the screen. I told my mom later that the baby was a drama queen and just wanted to keep her mommy worrying about her all the time. I was always scared because of the loss of the twins; I was always

Charise Marie

on edge thinking something bad would happen. I tried to think positive thoughts, but so many bad things had happened since the loss of the twins that all I could think about was that something bad would happen. I was worried most times while out by myself because I always felt faint. One afternoon I had been scheduled to go to my regular checkup and I got off public transportation and almost passed out. My fiancée had decided to stay home to do the baby's room, so I was on the bus alone in the early part of June. We all know how warm it can get in June.

My doctor had me scheduled for a C-section on July 6th. I tried to get her to change the date to July 4th or July 7th: July 4th is Independence Day, and July 7th sounds cute when you say 7/7/17, but she said, "No, we are keeping July 6th because it is the only day I am doing C-sections."

I had a severe asthma attack on June 24th, about two weeks before I was due. I went into the hospital that Saturday morning and they gave me a treatment. I felt okay enough to go home after receiving it. But my asthma flared back up when I got home. I told my fiancée later that night that I thought I needed to go back to the hospital because my breathing was getting difficult. She didn't want to drive down in that area because parking was a lot of money, so I took an Uber. She kept texting me to see if I had arrived: The driver was super slow.

I was admitted as soon as I arrived. My fiancée texted to ask what was going on, and I told her that they kept giving me treatment after treatment but that I still couldn't breathe. They gave me an X-ray and asked me to fill out papers just in case they had to deliver the baby while I

Pushing Through

was admitted. My fiancée came up to the hospital the next morning to check on me.

I was in the hospital from Saturday until Tuesday. It was one of the worst asthmatic hospital stays I have ever experienced. It took them a long time to get the medications to me. I thought to myself, If you know the medicine works and will not harm the baby, then don't have me sit around for hours not being able to breath. The doctors came in my room that Tuesday morning and I told them that I was ready to go. I was getting frustrated because although they wanted to make sure the baby and I were alright, I felt as if they just wanted to keep me there. My fiancée Tiny stayed with me the whole time. Since no one was in the bed next to me, they allowed her to sleep in that hospital bed.

Charise Marie

"You never know how strong you are until being strong is the only choice you have." – Cayla Mills

Pushing Through

Chapter Ten:

Disturbance

On Thursday, July 6th, I was in the hospital at 6:00 a.m. prepping for my C-section. I went into the delivery room around 8:00 a.m., and by 8:52 a.m., she was born. My rainbow baby was here! (A rainbow baby is when a baby is born after a previous pregnancy loss.) Thank you, God! Thank you! She was 8 pounds, 7 ounces, and 20 inches long. She was absolutely beautiful; just breathtaking. Thank you, God! I was extremely tired so I kept telling my fiancée, Tiny, to take a ton of pictures and to hold our baby. She was a tad bit scared to hold her because the baby was so small, but she did. She held her first then gave her to me. I felt like I was going to drop her, so I told my fiancée to take her and keep an eye on her. I kissed the baby, got stitched up, and went to the recovery room.

My fiancée and I were so excited that the baby was finally here. "Baby Firecracker" had sure given her mother a long nine months' worth of worrying about her. I had been skeptical about breastfeeding, but I learned a lot about it and decided to do it. As soon as they took me into the recovery room, I began learning how to breastfeed her. It wasn't as hard as I thought it would be. She slept most of the day so feeding her like the nurses instructed was difficult since she was not waking up for me. My fiancée was in contact with a bunch of our friends. They came to the

Charise Marie

hospital on the first night, and on Friday night as well. I was taken aback by how many of them came as soon as she was born, but I was excited that they wanted to see our baby. I just kept hearing my Pop Pop saying, "Make sure they wash their hands, Mook." They all came in and washed their hands and used the blankets to hold her. They never kissed her or anything like that. I was a little pissed off and became very quiet when they started making remarks about her appearance, though. She looks Asian. "Who was your sperm donor?" and other little remarks were said about her complexion and hair. I think my best friend, Heaven, was the only one who picked up on me shutting down because she got quiet and looked at me. The comments made me angry. I told all of them to stop saying things about my baby, but I guess they thought I was just joking, so I remained quiet because I didn't want my attitude to flare up at a joyous time.

The baby was released on Sunday, and we took a cab home. Once we arrived, an argument started between Tiny and me. I placed the baby on the couch, still in her car seat. My fiancée came over to me and asked if I was going to take her out of her car seat. I said, "No, I'm going to let her sleep." Tiny said that the doctor said she must lie flat, and I said, "No, she's fine."

Tiny said, "But the doctor said you must lie her flat," and I said, "I just told you she is fine. The doctor was saying to lie her flat when it comes to her lying in her crib. Why are you questioning what I said? I'm her mother, I won't let anything harm her."

She said, "But when we were in the hospital—"

Pushing Through

I cut her off and asked her, "Are you questioning my parenting?" It really felt like she was questioning my parenting, and I was becoming pissed off. I screamed at her: "I'm the one in pain from this C-section!" She walked out of the room to put some things away and I texted a few friends and told them to come and get Tiny before I snapped because she was starting her shit and we had just gotten home. Heaven popped by with her friend while my son was helping me put the playpen together. Tiny asked Heaven to help her understand if what she said to me was wrong. Heaven told her, "You have to understand that Charise is a mommy again. After the loss she experienced with the twins, she's going to be a little more emotional about things and feel like she's being attacked because, let's face it, she did just have a baby and that will have her hormones out of whack. And her experiencing the loss of the twins won't make it better for her either."

Heaven's friend chimed in and said, "I've known Charise for more than fifteen years, and she can be a little over the top, but she means no harm. She may have come off the wrong way when she responded to you, but if she feels like she is being attacked, she will become very defensive. I do know that about her." They told Tiny that nothing was wrong with what she asked me, but that maybe she should not have pressed the issue so many more times after I gave her an answer stating the baby was okay. We both stood there crying as neither one of us meant any harm. The fight had just happened.

We took the baby to her first doctor's appointment the next day. As we drove out on the street from our garage, a car went around a beverage truck and slammed into the

Charise Marie

back of our car on the side the baby was on. The entire time Tiny and I have been in a relationship, and the entire time Tiny has been driving, we have never been in an accident. But as soon as we put the baby in the car, here came this fool. He sped off and I was distraught. I called my family and told them. I was frantic because he could have killed my baby. The doctor told me that she was fine from the accident, but she had lost a few ounces since being born. I became concerned about it; I had never heard of a baby losing weight after birth, but people said it was normal. The breastfeeding consultant came in and we spoke a lot about breastfeeding. I was irritated because they had five people in the room while my breast was out and the nurse was explaining to me how to breastfeed squirting milk. They asked us to come back in three days for another checkup and wanted to focus on breastfeeding again.

    The next morning when I awoke, I went to the bathroom and immediately started crying. I found myself upset over a lot of stuff that had happened the past few days since the baby was born. The breastfeeding, the name-calling about her looks, and to top it off, the three-year anniversary of the death of the twins. Everything seemed to have hit me at once. My fiancée came in the bathroom and asked me why was I crying. I guess I had been in the bathroom too long. I quickly told her that I didn't want to talk about it, and she asked me why. I just kept crying with my head down and finally told her (after she asked three times) that I felt sad about how everyone was talking about the way she looks. Plus, the doctors made me feel like my breast milk wasn't working for her. Tiny said, "Little mama is beautiful; why would you be upset about what our friends were saying about her looks?" I said that she looked like a boy to me.

Pushing Through

Tiny said "She's gorgeous, babe."

I went in the room and explained to her how hurt the doctors made me feel. I never wanted to breastfeed until I learned more about it and heard that it was a wonderful thing, and now it seemed like it's not working for her. She just said, "Pray on it, babe."

We found out during the baby's next few appointments that the baby kept losing more ounces. I was scared because it made me feel like I wasn't giving my baby enough breast milk. I discussed it with Tiny. We talked about giving her formula as the only other option to make us both feel better and like she was getting what she needed. I had purchased some formula a few days before she was born just in case I didn't like breastfeeding. Once I started giving her the formula, she began picking up weight. I told my fiancée that I wanted to take the baby to another hospital to get a second opinion about her weight and giving her formula. Tiny said that she didn't want to go that far out to the other hospital and to give this children's hospital another chance. I looked at her like she was crazy. "What do you mean you don't want to go that far to another hospital to make sure our daughter is okay?" Tiny said that she didn't want to drive twenty to thirty minutes away from where we live when the children's hospital is only five minutes away. I was pissed, but I left it alone. I texted two friends and told them how angry I was at her comment, and they both said that they would drive me and the baby if need be because the baby's well-being came first.

The three-year anniversary of the twins' death came around shortly after I had my baby girl—three weeks after

Charise Marie

to be exact. I got up the morning before the anniversary, and Tiny sent me a text message saying she was praying that I was okay because she knows July is a hard month for me. She said that she hoped that remembering the twin angels and having a baby girl in July would help bring happiness to the month. She then told me that she loved me. I thanked her. I also explained that that's why I wanted her born in July to turn it around some. It's still hard, though.

Later that morning, our friend Nic asked my fiancée for help with planning her girlfriend, Irene's, birthday gathering. My fiancée said sure. Tiny was on the phone as Irene and Nic were having a disagreement, and Tiny put the phone on the bed and grabbed me and kissed me out of nowhere. She told me that the kiss was what I'd been missing, and I looked at her like, "What was that for?" We hadn't been affectionate for a while, so the kiss was a bit of a shock. I realized that maybe she saw how affectionate I was with the baby. I hugged and kissed the baby a whole lot. She got back on the phone and asked if they wanted to come over later that evening for crabs because Irene was upset with Nic; Tiny thought it would be a nice way to cheer up Irene. I looked at her like she was crazy. I was the one sitting there mourning the third anniversary of the death of our twins, and she's trying to help our friend cheer up her girlfriend. She said, "No, babe, it's not what you think." I just said nothing.

She later said, "Babe, we are going to help Nic pick out a cake tomorrow." I wanted to rip off her face so badly. She was helping Nic cheer up her girlfriend and planning her birthday gathering while I was crying and trying to understand what's going on with me. I just kept my feelings to

Pushing Through

myself and didn't say much because if I did I would be told that I was starting shit.

Irene invited us over for a seafood night on that Saturday and a last-minute cookout on that Sunday. When we got up Saturday morning, the baby was screaming, and I didn't understand why. At first I thought she was extra sleepy. When I looked at her body, however, I saw that she was curled up like it was her stomach. Then, while we were on the phone with Nic and Irene planning the seafood night, the baby started screaming again. There was a comment made by one of them saying, "Oh no, y'all about to go to the hospital. You know she's going to be extra cautious and overprotective." I told my fiancée to hang up the phone before I got pissed off. I told Tiny, "This is our baby and she's not feeling well, so yes, I am going to be overprotective and no, going to have seafood is not as important as taking our baby to the hospital to make sure she is okay, so get dressed." I threw on my clothes, but Tiny was upstairs taking forever. The baby was screaming in my arms, and I was panicking. I yelled up to her and asked what was taking so long, and she said, "I'm getting dressed." I got mad and said I was going to take a cab to the hospital because she was taking too long. When we finally got there, the doctor just looked at my daughter and told us to change her formula. I was livid! I looked at Tiny and said, "See, this is the shit I'm talking about. This is why I've been wanting to go to another hospital for a second opinion. How do you look at her and just say to change her formula?"

She said, "Well, let's go to the other hospital." I agreed.

The doctor looked at me and said, "Well, what do you

Charise Marie

want me to do?"

I said, "You can give her an X-ray to see what's wrong with her. Do your job!"

They finally took us down to get an X-ray. We found out that she had a belly full of gas, so they gave us a prescription for some infant gas-relief drops.

The next day came and I told my fiancée that I did not want to go to the cookout that our friend was having, and she got mad that she would have to go alone. I just didn't feel comfortable going with my baby not feeling well. Plus, she was a screaming baby at that. Tiny and I got into an argument, and I just told her to go and have a good time. I was angry that she wanted to hang out after we just took our baby to the hospital, but I left it alone. I personally thought that she should be home with our daughter instead of running the street. She said she thought the baby was fine since she wasn't screaming, and she left. I texted her while she was at the cookout and asked her to bring the baby's car seat in the house once she came home. She texted me back asking what for, and that when I get mad I shouldn't act petty toward her. I responded by saying that I needed it, that's what for. She called me, and I was very irritated. I told her not to call me when she's around people when they could overhear our conversation. I said, "You complain about carrying all the stuff in the house since I had a C-section, so I don't ask you to bring the car seat in. You complain about carrying all the groceries and the baby, so I leave the car seat in there. I want to adjust the straps on it so the baby sits comfortably and correctly in it." She agreed to bring it in, but when she walked in the house later

Pushing Through

she didn't have it and she told me that I was being petty. I flipped out. We started having an argument and she called me "crazy" and "nutty." She jumped on the phone with Nic and Irene and told them that I was acting crazy, and I told her get off the phone and to stop talking about me. She didn't get off the phone, and I kept hearing her talk badly about me. I heard her say, "She's acting crazy; I think she's dealing with that post stuff." I put the baby on the bed and I jumped up and grabbed my taser and threated to zap her ass. She started screaming for me to get away from her, and I said, "Did you just call me nutty and crazy? I'll show you crazy! Now get off the phone and stop calling me names!" She held the fan up and blocked me from zapping her. If I really wanted to zap her, I could have. I have longer arms than she does. But I never turned it on. I told her to get out of my house and that our relationship was over. This was not the first time I told her that it was over and to get out. I'd probably told her 6,379 times it was over and to get out. I grabbed the baby and went downstairs where I placed the baby in her playpen.

    I slept on the couch that night. I was up most of it since the baby screamed for two hours on and off with her gas pains. I became even more enraged because Tiny never came downstairs to ask if the baby was okay. She told me the next morning that she was still mad at me for pulling a taser on her. I didn't care if I used it or not; our daughter was sick and Tiny had stayed in bed. I was mad. The two friends, Nic and Irene, she had been on the phone with the night before both contacted me the next day to tell me to breathe and keep calm because they had never heard me like that before. They were concerned. Irene asked if I was feeling okay, and I told her no. I told her that I was angry

Charise Marie

that Tiny brought up my son during our argument. She said that he hadn't seen his sister since she was born, and all he wanted to do was see his girlfriend. Kids are off limits in arguments and she knows that. He's eighteen. Tiny then mentioned that some other friends hadn't been by to see the baby either. I told her that I didn't care who came to see her. Irene asked me whether I was having a breakdown the night before. She was scared for me because of the way I sounded on the phone. She said that I had been way over the top and, as a friend, she thought I should see my therapist because she believed I had been displaying signs of postpartum depression (PPD) since the baby was born. She also said that she thought I should make an appointment because I had suffered from PTSD after the loss of the twins. I told her I was just tired of the relationship and everything being blamed on me the past seven years. We were both at fault for things that happened. My other friend Nic contacted me as well and asked whether I was mad at her. I told her no. My main issue was with Tiny, and besides, no one wanted to be around a sick, screaming baby, especially their own.

A few days passed when Tiny and I talked calmly to each other. But that quickly changed. We saw our therapist on Wednesday of that week and explained to her what happened. She asked to see us separately over the next two weeks. She asked Tiny if it was okay to see me because we transitioned from paying a cash fee to putting everything on Tiny's insurance. Tiny agreed. The therapist wanted to see Tiny in two weeks and me the week after that. Every night since our first blow up, I slept downstairs on the couch. I slept in our bed a few of the days and I got up every day and went downstairs just to keep things calm and to

Pushing Through

have a little bit of space between us. Tiny came downstairs, the day after the appointment, and asked if I wanted to take a ride with her to run some errands. I said "Yes, maybe some hot, sticky, muggy August weather would be good for us all," and we laughed. It was hot outside, so she had the air on very high in the truck because I was sitting in the back with the baby. She asked me if I was going to Irene's birthday gathering. I told her that I didn't feel comfortable leaving the baby just yet. Tiny had asked my mom the week before to watch the baby while we went to the birthday dinner. My mom had agreed. My family and friends already knew that, because of the loss of twins, I would have a hard time leaving this baby alone. It was a process for me that I had to get through, but let's face it, she was only three weeks old. Tiny asked whether I wanted to take the baby with me, and I told her no. She then said that everyone would be coupled up. I told her no, everyone attending would not be coupled up; a few people weren't in relationships. Besides, what does that have to do with the baby? She told me I was being selfish, and I asked her how. She said because everyone would be there with their mate, and she'd be there by herself. I said, "I don't want to leave the baby, and I certainly don't want to take the baby in a restaurant around all sorts of people." She pulled off the road and said that when we got in the house we were going to call Irene and Nic so we could discuss this because I needed to be exposed. I was pissed. Exposed about what? When we got back in the house, I texted them and told them that Tiny was about to call. She did. I ignored all of them. I told Tiny I had nothing to say; I did not feel like talking to anyone. I heard Tiny say that she was about to expose me for the person I really was: "Charise doesn't want to come to your birthday party because she's being petty, and she doesn't want your

Charise Marie

friend to hold the baby because she's afraid she might drop her because she has Tourette's." I looked at her like she was crazy because I never said that to her. I jumped up, placed the baby down for her nap, and went in the kitchen. Tiny followed me. I told her to please get away from me and to stop following me because she was agitating me. We went back into the living room and I put my headphones on. Tiny told Nic and Irene, "She's ignoring me and doesn't want me to tell you guys that she doesn't want to come because she is afraid your friend will drop the baby." I looked at her like, are you serious right now? I heard Irene say that she didn't want me to take her out for her birthday because she didn't like what was being said. I turned the music up louder so I couldn't hear what they were saying. I felt like all three of them were bashing me and attacking my character, so I got up and went in the kitchen to heat up my food. I heard Tiny say more about me when I turned the music off. I snapped. She kept saying, "I told y'all she's crazy, and you're right, she is dealing with that post stuff you were talking about. I told you she's been walking around here crying all crazy." I grabbed the longest kitchen knife I had and ran in the dining room by my staircase. She was in the living room on the couch. She screamed, "Oh my gosh, y'all, now she has a knife."

I said, "If you say one more thing about me, I'm coming over there with this knife and I'm not playing with you this time. Stop talking about me. Why do you think it's okay as my mate to throw me under the bus? If I don't want my new three-week-old baby out running the street, then you should respect that. Both of them as mothers should understand that and be telling you that. Instead, y'all on the phone talking about me acting crazy. Stop calling me cra-

Pushing Through

zy because I'm dealing with things. Stop talking about me before I come over there after your ass. I'm not going to tell you again."

The baby and I slept downstairs in the living room again and I texted my girlfriend Simone (Sassy), the baby's godmother. I told her that if something happened to me, that Tiny and I had been arguing a lot. I then said that I was going to book a room for the weekend so I could clear my head before I did something I would regret. Sassy called me and asked what was going on. I cried and told her that Tiny was verbally attacking me, and I was picking up weapons to physically attack her. I was hurt and angry. Why was going out so important to her? She knew once we had this baby that we wouldn't be able to run the street like we normally did. I told her to go without me, and I guess because we are always together, that that's the issue she's having, but our daughter isn't feeling well. How come she doesn't get that? Sassy said, "Please don't pick up anything else. If you need to come stay with me for a few days, please come stay." I told her that I didn't want to put anyone out of their way in their own home, and that I'd just go to the hotel until Sunday. She said that she didn't want me spending all that money because I'm unemployed and have to be smart with my money. I told her I was fine. The money wasn't a major issue for me; it was only $250 from Friday to Sunday. I just needed to get out of the house to clear my mind because I couldn't keep snapping at Tiny. I felt like she didn't care about me or the baby. Why was she agitating me? I shouldn't be feeling like this.

Friday morning arrived and I gave the baby a bath. I took the baby in the bedroom and Tiny told me that I had wo-

Charise Marie

ken her up. I apologized to her and asked if she wanted me to go out of the room. The television was on so I guess she fell back asleep. I just dressed the baby. When Tiny woke up, I asked her very nicely to get the baby's car seat, and she asked if I was going somewhere. I told her yes. I needed to get out of the house before anything else happened. She said, "I'm not getting anything," and I said, "I'm asking you nicely because I'm trying to avoid an argument." I went downstairs to feed the baby and to wait for her to get the car seat. Tiny asked me where I was going, and I just told her that I was going away for a few days to clear my mind. She said, "I'm not getting anything because you're not taking the baby away from me."

I said, "I'm not going to say it again. I'm asking you nicely to get the baby's car seat. It's not your property, so go and get it before I get my bat and bust out your car windows to get it."

She said, "You touch my car and I'm calling the cops!"

I said, "Just please get the car seat. Thank you."

She stood at the top of the stairs and yelled down at me. She said, "That's why I told our friends about you yesterday with your insecure ass."

I said, "What?"

She said, "I told them you didn't want to come to the birthday party because you are insecure over that girl."

I put the baby in the playpen, went in the kitchen, and

Pushing Through

grabbed the knife again. Tiny flew into the bedroom. She stood at the top part of the left side of the bed, her side, and I stood at the bottom right side of the bed, my side. I said, "What did you say? You told them I was being insecure over who?"

She said, "No, what I said was you were acting funny about the girl holding your baby."

I said, "No, no, no, that's not what you just stood at the top of the step and screamed." I started jabbing the knife into my comforter and crying. I saw nothing but red in front of me. I said, "I swear, all I want to do is hurt you right now. Stop saying things about me. I said that to you yesterday. Get the baby's car seat now! I'm am on the verge of killing you. Get the car seat now! Right now!" I screamed. She said, "Put the knife down."

I said, "Girl, I'm not playing with you; my head is about to bust because all of this is crazy to me."

She said, "You are crazy."

I said, "Call me crazy one more time, ugh." Then I said to myself, *No, Charise, leave; please leave now.* I slammed the bedroom door, put the knife back in the kitchen, and then jumped in the shower and cried and prayed to God to get me out of the house before I lost my rights as a mother by going to jail. I tried to figure out if Tiny was mad at me for something and, if so, what? Maybe she's mad at me because she bought two different sets of concert tickets and we didn't go to either concert. I told her when she purchased them that it would be just two and three weeks after I had

Charise Marie

my C-section, so I may not be up to going. She sold the tickets, but maybe she was mad at me for not being able to go.

I got out of the shower, and Tiny had the car seat on the chair in the living room. I got dressed in the bathroom and told my mom and Sassy that I needed to leave because I had picked up a knife again. They calmed me down on the phone. I got a text message from Nic before I left asking me why I was so angry and saying they needed to talk to me. I just kindly said that I was all talked out and exhausted. She asked whether I was talking to them or not, and I said my friends advised me to leave things alone for my own sanity. Irene said that they didn't do anything to me, and I needed to see a doctor really soon. She said she was trying to hear my side of the story. I said, "I'm just pissed and need to leave before something bad happens." She wished me well and said once again to please call my therapist. I hated the fact that she kept yelling at me on the phone and telling me to call my doctor like I was crazy, so I chose not to speak with them over the phone. Was that where Tiny was getting this from?

I called my mom once I arrived at the hotel. She told me she was on the phone with Tiny and she would call me back. I unpacked our stuff while I waited. I had only brought a two-liter bottle of Pepsi and some cherries with me to eat. I didn't have to worry about the baby's milk as I was breast-feeding her. I called Sassy to let her know that I was okay and in the hotel. I just needed to clear my mind because I didn't understand what's going on between Tiny and me. I told her I had already read stories about PPD. Could that be what I had? I asked her, "Who wants to go around say-

Pushing Through

ing they are depressed? Certainly not me." I didn't want to claim having PPD, especially since I was diagnosed with PTSD after the loss of the twins. I didn't want anything else added to my medical record. I had been through enough already.

I started thinking about how I was not eating right. I drank Pepsi all day and barely ate full meals. I had cereal in the morning and fruit throughout the day or a hot sausage here or there. I had already felt my pressure spiking, so I had to find a way to keep as calm as possible. I just laid on the bed thinking about how much I loved Tiny, but I could not for the life of me understand how we had gotten to this point after seven years together. I'm the kind of person who has a hard time expressing my feelings or crying over situations, but here I was in the hotel room just crying and crying. Luckily, the baby was asleep, so I had time to reflect on the past few days. When I talked to my mom, she asked me what was going on. I told her the story, and she told me that Tiny had told her the story. She asked what I was thinking with the weapons, and I told her that using them was never my intention. I was just so hurt with the way things were going that I wanted to hurt Tiny because I felt like she kept verbally attacking me. I told my mom that I never came close to Tiny with the weapons, and my mom told me she didn't have any bail money and was not raising any kids. We laughed, and I said, "Yes, mom, I know." She told me that she had told my son what was going on. He later came up to stay the night with me and the baby.

Saturday came, which was the day the birthday party for Irene was planned. I got up, and my son and I ate breakfast at the hotel since it was free. I ordered Chinese food for

Charise Marie

lunch and tried to eat the rest of it for dinner. I decided not to attend the birthday dinner because I needed time away to get myself together. Once my son left early that afternoon, I laid on the bed crying and praying to God to fix the situation. I knew I loved Tiny, but staying in this type of relationship was not what I wanted, so God had to be the one to fix the situation. *God, please fix this. I don't want to lose our family. We fought too hard to get pregnant, and you took our twins. Now you blessed us with this beautiful little girl. God, please fix this. We should be at the happiest time in our relationship with our brand-new rainbow baby.* I didn't know what God was doing to me, but I felt so out of whack with everything. It was hard for me to explain, and I didn't want to talk about it most of the time.

When Sunday came, I checked out and went home. Tiny came downstairs and kissed the baby as she was lying in the playpen. She asked if we could talk, and we went in the kitchen and had a conversation. She asked where I had been all weekend. I pulled out the receipt for the hotel. I asked why she didn't contact me to see if we were okay, and she said she wanted to give me the space I needed. I told her I saw her on social media at our friend's party having a nice time, and she said no one asked about me. I laughed and said, "That's okay." We had a calm conversation about what was going on with us, and we said we would try to figure things out. I later sent her a text message apologizing for my actions toward her that past week. She thanked me. I started sleeping back up in our bedroom, but each day I continued to come downstairs as I thought we still needed a little space.

In the middle of that week I was on the phone with a

Pushing Through

friend of Tiny's, Dani, who was going through a crisis. I was praying with her and for her. We then started talking about hooking her up with some of my single friends, and she told me her zodiac sign. I laughed. I said she would pair well with this sign and that sign. Tiny was upstairs getting ready for her doctor's appointment and must've overheard some of my conversation. She ran downstairs and asked me to place my call on mute. I did until she started accusing me of cheating on her with whomever I was on the phone with. I quickly unmuted the phone so her friend Dani could hear how she spoke to me. I told Tiny that I was not trying to hook up with the person on the phone; I was trying to set her up with a friend and was also praying for her. Dani was listening and just said, "Wow, I've never heard her speak that way. Just tell her it's me."

I told Dani, "That's because no one knows what goes on behind closed doors. Some days it's her talking nasty to me, and other days it's me talking nasty to her."

Tiny must've thought about her accusation while she was at the clinic. She apologized to me when she arrived back home. I just said, "Thanks."

The weekend rolled around and Tiny said that she was going out for a bit and did I need her to get me something. She said that she might stop at the wholesale store. I looked at her like she was crazy as she doesn't usually go out without me, but I just said that I didn't need anything. She was gone from 11:00 a.m. to 5:30 p.m. Oh yes, I watched that clock because I wondered where she was for all those hours. I contacted a friend, who Tiny didn't like because she was tomboyish like she was, and invited her to get together so we could talk about our relationship drama. This friend and I had stopped speaking once Tiny told me she felt uncomfortable with us being friends. I had cut off my friendship with her to try and save my relationship. My friend told me she would get back to me once she got home. I gave the baby her bath and took my shower so we would be ready to go once my friend contacted me. She called around 7:30 p.m., and I told her give me until 8:00 to get our clothes on. I went upstairs to get dressed, and Tiny asked where was I going. I said, "Out for a bit."

She said, "At this time of night?"

I said, "Yes."

I got downstairs and Tiny smelled that I had sprayed on perfume. I did it because I had smelled like throw up from the baby being sick most of the day. Tiny followed me down the street even though I told her not to make a scene. She kept yelling at me saying that I better not be meeting who she thought. I got to the end of my block where my friend was waiting. She didn't have my exact address because I had never invited her over because Tiny didn't like her. She said she remembered that I lived across from the bowling alley. Tiny saw my friend and said, "Okay, I'm going to talk about this on social media." My friend and I just left. We went to the department store to exchange my friend's jeans, and she told me what she was going through with her partner and I gave her some advice. Once we were done at the department store, we drove all over the city and then back up to my area. She asked, "What's going on?" I told her that I didn't know what's going on between Tiny and me, and she just let me vent to her. Even though she knew

Pushing Through

Tiny never liked her, she said, "Mook, there's nothing out here for us in the gay community. Find a way to work it out if you can. Try to do therapy and talk to each other calmly. At the end of the day, it's hard to start over and find someone that's good for you. I know you two have been through your share of ups and downs, but y'all been together seven years and have a baby now. Y'all have to find a way to work it out. I don't condone what you did to her, and I understand you felt attacked, but you have to find a way to work it out if that's what you want to do."

I told my friend that I loved Tiny but just didn't understand why this was happening with us right now.

She said, "I'll say a prayer for you guys," and dropped me off at 10:00. I went in the house and heard Tiny get off the phone. I put the baby's stuff away and went upstairs. Tiny was finally starting to clean up her area. She said that she was packing to leave because I was cheating on her. I started putting the baby to sleep. I turned off the light on my side of the room as she had on the ceiling light and table lamp. She immediately screamed at me and said that I was picking on her by coming in and starting my shit, and I wouldn't let her pack peacefully. I looked at her and said, "What are you talking about now?"

She said, "You turned off the light knowing I was using it."

I said, "But it's on my side. The baby is asleep, and you have the ceiling light on."

She screamed at me again. I jumped up to grab my taser,

Charise Marie

but she had moved it. She said, "Oh yeah, I moved it away from you."

I said, "So you knew you were going to start something with me, is that why you moved it?" She grabbed her phone and called Nic again telling her I was acting crazy.

I said, "Ef you and ef them too. Get off the phone before I punch you." She started screaming at me, and I said to stop screaming around the baby. Then I jumped out of bed and told her to get off the phone. I told her I was going to grab the bat in the corner if she kept on screaming around the baby. She finally left the room and stayed downstairs.

We had a volunteer event the next morning to cook breakfast for the families with children in the hospital. Tiny had placed a post about me on social media at 3:00 a.m., but she blocked it from me so I couldn't see it. A few people told me about it. I was pissed. We said we would never place our personal relationship business on social media. She left at 6:00 that morning to go to the volunteer place which was five minutes from our house. I jumped in a cab at 8:00 to get to the home to volunteer. I took the baby with me. I arrived, and we barely said two words to each other, but we cooked for the families. I asked Kelly, who volunteered with us, if she could take me home. She said yes. But once we were leaving, Tiny said she was going home and would take us with her. I thanked her once we arrived home. We were exhausted from the night before, so she stayed upstairs while I stayed downstairs. She said, "I know we are both tired from last night, so if you want to come lay in the bed with the baby, I can come downstairs." I thanked her, but the baby and I stayed downstairs. I went in the kitchen later

Pushing Through

and just prayed to God for guidance. I said, "God, I don't know if this is a seven-year itch thing that I hear about, or if this is the end of our relationship, but we need to get this figured out. God, fix this situation. I don't know what to do. I don't want anything to happen to either one of us, so I need guidance. Guide me down the right path."

The next day was the baby's six-week appointment, and mine with my doctor. I expressed to Tiny that I did not want her to attend the baby's doctor appointment because we kept bumping heads and I didn't want tension at her appointment, but once I was home I would let her know what they said. We had another argument, and I just got dressed and left. I called my mom on the way to the appointment and told her I would be coming to stay with her for the next month until Tiny moved out of my house.

She said, "Okay, your son has moved some things out of the room. There's no television or cable in the room, so you can watch it in my room." I told her that would be okay. At this point I needed peace and quiet to reflect on my next steps. I packed our stuff once I came home from our doctors' appointments. Tiny asked where was I going, and I just told her that I would leave until she's done packing because I was told that she placed another post on social media. People told me what she wrote: that I wasn't allowing her to pack peacefully, and I was out dating with my newborn baby. I told her, "I don't appreciate you blocking me from the post to bash me on social media. I'm not dating anyone, and I never messed with you when you were packing. So, to allow you to pack in peace, I will leave my house. Once you are gone on Labor Day weekend like you said, then I will come back." She asked if she could pick up the

Charise Marie

baby, and I said yes. She picked her up and said she would miss her and kissed her a few times. I caught a cab and left for my mom's house. My son met me and the baby outside because I needed help carrying clothes for both of us for a few days, her formula, and other little electronics to keep us busy. I gave my mom the baby, and she told me to get settled. I texted a handful of friends to let them know that I was at my mom's house until Tiny left my home. Most of them told me that I was crazy for leaving my own house instead of putting her out, and I just said, "No, I'm just going to be nice and give her time to get her things so she can go." Everyone said that they were praying for us, and for me to focus on the new baby girl and try to get myself together. Tiny texted me the next two days to say hi to the baby to tell her that she loved and missed her, and I responded by sending her a picture of the baby saying she missed her too. I had nothing to do in the room at my mom's, so I reflected a lot. I cried and tried to understand how we had gotten to where we were. One thing I noticed was that the whole situation was making me more in touch with my emotional side. I didn't usually cry, but lately that's all I'd been doing.

Pushing Through

"Sometimes, Life will kick you around, but sooner or later you will realize you're not just a survivor. You're a warrior and you're stronger than anything life throws your way." – Brooke Davis

Charise Marie
Eleven: The Storm

    I went to my very first appointment at my local clinic since a few people were telling me that I was displaying signs of postpartum depression. The clinics intake coordinator did an intake and wanted me to come back a few days later and I did. The intake coordinator told me I was diagnosed with postpartum depression, and she set me up with my first appointment to see the therapist and then to see the psychiatrist. One helps with the treatment plan, and the other gives medication. I told her that I did not want to be on medication at that time. I then received a phone call from our couple's therapist that Tiny and I were seeing. She told me that she had to cancel my appointment for that Wednesday, and I laughed. I said, "Tiny came to therapy yesterday and told you that she wants my appointment canceled." She didn't confirm or deny what I said. I told her how wrong I thought that was for both of them, because if I was suffering from postpartum depression, I needed help. She said she could recommend someone there for me to see, but I told her no, thank you. I already had my doctors arranged. I told my mom and a few close friends about the cancellation, and they all were upset that my therapist cut me out of Chapter therapy just to see Tiny by herself. She didn't even think that seeing me could help my situation. I felt like my sanity was being tested at this point, and they all thought the same thing. They were all really angry about the whole situation.

    I received a phone call from someone who told me that they saw Tiny posting pictures on social media. She was hanging out with people I thought were "our" friends. I

Pushing Through

deleted her and handful of people who claimed to be my friends, but who instead instantly took Tiny's side without being concerned about the baby or hearing my side of the story. I was upset that she was out partying with friends all weekend when I had asked her to take me to another clinic for a second opinion, and she told me the other clinic was too far. It felt like a stab in the back. Partying was more important to her than taking our daughter to get her well. I was even more angry because the places where she was partying were in the same vicinity as the hospital, and one place was even outside of the city. I don't like relying on rumors, but I saw the pictures posted on her social media page; someone sent them to me.

My girlfriend Sassy picked me up to go shopping for the baby as she was running out of fresh Gerber baby water and other items. I called Tiny and asked her if she was in the house and if she could unlock the basement door (we always kept it locked if we were in the house). She said she would come down and open it. I dropped off some of the items I could not fit at my mom's house in the kitchen at my house. We had a casual conversation. She told me what bills had come in and asked who took me to the store. I told her to look outside; it was our mutual friend, Sassy. We then got into a conversation about our relationship that turned into an argument. I asked her whether she wanted to be in a relationship with me; it felt like I was begging her. She said she didn't want to talk about it right then because she was still upset over some of the things I did to her with the weapons. I told her we needed to go to intense therapy, and she said we needed individual therapy. I reminded her that I'd been seeing my individual therapist for a few years. I asked her about our couple's therapist and what

Charise Marie

happened. She gave me a story about how the therapist felt like she was compromising her license by having me come in separately, and thought she may be fired. I told her that it was a lie and that she told her to cancel my appointment, and she told me that she wouldn't do that to me. I mentioned that we had been going to her for the last year on Tiny's insurance, and the therapist didn't think of her license then. I then stormed out because I started screaming at her. When we got outside, she and Sassy spoke. Sassy asked if we were okay, and I told her that I couldn't work out anything with Tiny. Tiny walked over to the car and looked at the baby who was asleep. She told Sassy that I was a bad friend because I had deleted our mutual friends on social media. I told her that I didn't care about those friends because they obviously didn't care about me. They hadn't contacted me, so why should I care about them? Did any of them contact me to ask how our sick daughter was doing? No. She told me that she was mad because now she had to move in with friends, and I didn't think of that when I was putting her out. She had no money, and I didn't offer to give her any money to move. Sassy asked her if there was anything she could do to help her; she wasn't on anybody's side but the baby's. Sassy said, "You two have to try to figure this out because you have a baby now," but Tiny just kept screaming that I was a bad friend. Sassy told her, "You need to stop having people in your ear and in your business. You two need to sit down and calmly figure this out." She offered to sit down with us, and Dani had as well, but Tiny told both of them no because she was still heated about our situation. Tiny also said she thought I was staying at the girl's house she thought I was messing around with. I just jumped in the car and sat there until they finished talking. When Tiny and Sassy were done, Sassy took me back to my

Pushing Through

mom's house and said she was praying hard for us to get it together for the baby. The baby needed both of us; we had fought too hard to have her after losing all the other babies. I just put my head down and was quiet for a while; I never thought we would be here. Over the seven years we were together, there were times I would get fed up with things and would get childish and tell her to get out or break up. I always told her that I went about it the wrong way thinking that if I told her those things that she would straighten up. Most of the time, she did. The sad thing is that we were both verbally abusive to one another. She was more so the first few years, and I was the last few years.

Tiny texted me and said she would be leaving on Tuesday of the next week. She would be back the following Monday to help my son put out the trash. I just said, "Okay." I had a doctor's appointment, so she asked if she could see the baby that next day. I agreed. Sassy and Dani drilled in me, "Mook, please do not bring up your relationship when you see her. She told us she doesn't want to talk about anything but the baby." I agreed, but told them that they didn't know her the way I do. I knew she would bring up the relationship. I planned to secretly record our conversation just like I recorded all the other times she and I had talked to each other like we were trash.

In the beginning, we actually had a calm conversation about the baby and about the things in the house. I then told her I had just changed the baby, made her a new bottle, and left her wipes and burp cloths on the table. She looked at me and asked where I was going, and I said I was going to go to the store, but since it's raining, I was going to go upstairs so they could spend some time together. She said

Charise Marie

she was ready to finally talk.

    We had a calm conversation about how we'd been together for seven years and should be able to talk to each other. Then she said, "I just didn't want to have a conversation before. I thought once we were less angry with one another, then we should have been able to sit down and talk calmly." I made her a plate of my baked ziti I had cooked the night before because I knew she loved it, and she said she'd take it with her because she had just eaten at work. I wrapped it up and gave her a glass of juice. She wanted to talk then, and I said "No, I was told that you only wanted to talk about the baby," and she said, "Let's talk and stop playing these games." She asked if there was anything going on that she should know about, and I told her that our mutual friends believed that I should tell her my real feelings, and that this whole situation had nothing to do with her hanging out with friends. It was about how I really felt about us and how hurt I was about the past. I told her, "The crazy thing is, my friends have never heard me be this vulnerable with them, and they think we need to talk. I need to be as honest with you about my feelings as much as possible." She said that she didn't understand how I changed from thinking things being said were funny before the baby was born to being mad about them after. She said, "I made you my priority, and I lost me." She said that I wasn't hanging out with my friends, and I neglected other things in my life. I was selfish, she said. Every time I had been sick or going through something, she had been there for me, but when she had doctors' appointments, I didn't ask about them. I looked at her like she was crazy. I asked her all the time how her appointments went; I just didn't ask specific questions like she wanted. Me asking how her appointment

Pushing Through

went summed it up, but she thought that she'd always been there for me and my needs only. She said she gave up because she felt like she was the only one fighting for our relationship. It's not that I got us multiple therapists for the whole seven years or tried changing who I was. No, that's not me fighting for our relationship, just her. She said she was mad because I didn't fight for her when she was leaving, and that's what she was looking for me to do this time. Instead, I just let her leave.

Apparently, her giving me the dates she was leaving had been my opportunity to say that I wanted to work things out; I should have fought for her. She said she was calling my bluff because she thought I never believed that she would leave. She said me picking up the weapons was too much for her; my actions made her feel like I hated her. She felt like I disrespected her by going out with my tomboy friend because she didn't like the girl. I then told Tiny that she was correct about saying that I laughed at things that were said before the baby was born, but after she was born a lot of stuff did change. I told her that I wouldn't be evaluated until the next day, but a lot of people thought I was dealing with postpartum depression. I told her if I was dealing with PPD, that was probably the reason why I didn't think anything was funny. I then told her how hurt I was that she said going to the other hospital for a second opinion was too far. She said she never told me no, that she just didn't have money for gas or parking. I said, "But you found it easy to go to a cookout and travel to all those other places within the city with friends. Why didn't you care enough about taking the baby to another clinic?" She claimed that once the baby came, I got mad at her for every little thing; I was sabotaging our relationship. I told Tiny

Charise Marie

that I got pissed when she put earplugs in one night when the baby was up crying. She told me I was clueless because she's never had a baby before, and I made a mountain out of a molehill. I put too many expectations on her with being a new mommy. Plus, she wears earplugs most nights. She said she felt like I nitpicked everything. She said I had been very petty when I changed the locks on her and she couldn't enter the house or wash her clothes in the washing machine she had purchased. She said I never put her first, and my only concern was for my daughter. I had already been neglecting her over the years, and once the baby came, it was all about me and the baby and not about me, her, and the baby.

Tiny did the majority of the talking the whole five hours we talked. That was normal for us, though, because most of the time I felt like I could never get my point across because she talked so much. I usually ignored her. She said that she had been honest with me when she said she wasn't going to stay up late all the time with the baby. She needed her rest. Our therapist told Tiny that she had to change that attitude because I would get burned out really quickly and start to resent her if I was the only one getting up at night. She said she hated it every time I posted on social media that my only concern was the baby when I should've said my only concern was with her and the baby, and I said, "What about my son? I love all three of you." But in her eyes, once someone pointed out that I shouldn't say the baby was my only concern, she saw issue with it. She never said anything about it until then. She then asked if she could see the baby on Tuesdays and Thursdays because she would be in the area leaving a late-day appointment. I told her that yes, that was fine. She said she wanted to visit whatever day she

Pushing Through

chose on the weekend. I told her that I still needed some time and space, so some days I would not want to be around her.

Later, Tiny told me that I should have fought for our relationship since I broke up with her; that I shouldn't be listening to people telling me to leave her. She said she wanted us to start building a friendship, which was something we never really had. We then got on the topic of our friends again. She told me the people I stopped talking to supported me and brought gifts for the baby shower. I asked whether I should give them back. I didn't like how they were hanging out with Tiny like they were taking her side when none of them had contacted me to ask how our daughter was doing. They didn't have to pretend to like me anymore or even care about my well-being, but they should at least contact me through text message to ask how the baby was doing. She said that I was pushing our friends away, and I was wrong because I was not a good friend. She said they never did anything to me, and just because I was going through something, I shouldn't push people away. I told her that I didn't do one-sided friendships. Why should I call, text, or send a smoke signal to friends when they go through something, when they don't return the favor and contact me when something goes wrong with me? She said that some of the people I'm still friends with aren't good friends anyway because they flirted with her while we were in a relationship among other things. She then said that some of our friends didn't deserve me deleting them via social media. I shouldn't have stopped talking to them because they came and helped with the baby shower, ate lunch with us, and went to various events of mine that I hosted. I should not have pushed them away. She said I needed to

Charise Marie

learn when right is right and wrong is wrong, and I was wrong for pushing them away. I said, "You are harping on people spending money on the baby shower, how about they ask about the baby?" She said that someone needed to tell me how ungrateful I sounded when I said I'd give the gifts back since it's all about them spending money. She said it's funny because I was going through something and I was pushing people out of my life, and the main person I pushed out was her over petty stuff instead of saying, "Hey, I'm going through something; would you like for me to explain what is going on?" I told her that I tried telling her and that she called friends saying that I was acting crazy even when I was just crying. She said that I should've never been listening to my single friends because they were miserable; I should be talking to those in relationships who are happy. I needed to see if the people who said negative stuff or that we should split up were in relationships that are happy. I needed to see if they had been through a breakup. Some people applaud when you break up because they want a chance with you or your mate. She asked whether I was ready to work on us being friends, and I told her that I didn't want to be her friend, that I wanted to be her wife. She said that we needed to work on a friendship first and pray that the Creator puts us back into having a better relationship. She said that I was a handful, and that I needed to learn to not be petty. She asked if she could stick to the days we discussed earlier, and I told her that I just needed to know ahead of time which weekend day she wanted to come. She said she should be able to come whenever she wanted, and I laughed. I told her that I would be out of town next week, and she said we needed to have the days locked in so she needed me to be available on the days. I told her that she needed to pick either Friday, Saturday or Sunday,

Pushing Through

and she said she would let me know which day when that day came. I told her that was not fair because now I would have to sit around and wait for her to tell me which day she wanted to come. What if I wanted to go to a movie or shopping? She said none of that was more important than her bonding with the baby, so I needed to make time for her to see the baby when she wanted. I told her that I would not sit around waiting for her to decide on which day. If I was going to be out of the house, she could come on another day. She said I was being petty. She said it was okay for her to run the street with friends, and that I was the problem in this relationship. I told her that I was going to Atlantic City for a few days, and she accused me of going with someone. She started screaming at me. She told me that I needed to stay in the house with a newborn, and I said, "But it's okay for you to run the street." She said that she's single, so she can do whatever she wants. I told her then she didn't need to worry about what or who I was doing since we were both single. She told me I was petty when I attended the appointment that was made for me when I should have asked for another day so she could come see the baby. Tiny also said I was being unfair to her by not allowing her to see the baby because I was planning on going out of town. I could play single on days she didn't come see the baby. I just laughed because now she thought that I needed to schedule my life around her visiting the baby when she wanted. I finally just caved in and said I would be available on whatever days she picked. I didn't want to argue with her anymore.

    I had plans on Labor Day weekend with family members who hadn't had a chance to see the baby yet. If it rained, we would not go. I told Tiny that I would not be available that weekend, and she said that she wanted to come see

Charise Marie

her. She didn't understand how I had plans from morning to night. I shouldn't be making plans all day. I told her I would be home after 7:00 p.m., and she said that's all day and that her seeing the baby should have nothing to do with my plans. She could spend time with the baby while I'm out "doing me." I told her I had canceled my plans since I heard it was going to rain, so she could come whenever she wanted; she just had to let me know which day. She left, and for the next few days we sent constant text messages back and forth to one another asking how each other was doing and saying we were praying for our situation and hoping for a better outcome. I also sent her pictures and videos of the baby when she was up at 4:00 a.m. for her feedings, which is the time Tiny gets up for work.

The Friday before Labor Day weekend arrived and Tiny called to ask what I was doing, and I said I was on my way to the movies. She flipped out. She said, "I told you that I wanted to see the baby on the weekends."

I said, "You never asked for today, so I got up and I'm on my way to enjoy a movie." She automatically accused me of being with someone else. I told her it was just me and the baby who was sleeping in the carrier on me. She asked which movie and what time it was playing because she was coming to get me, and I better not be with anyone else. I told her the information because I didn't want to argue with her. I said, "Why would you come all the way up here?" She ignored me and hung up. She texted me forty-five minutes before the movie ended saying she was at the movie theater and had asked the guy at the front door what time the movie was over, and he gave her the information. I told her that once the movie was over, I was going to change the baby in

Pushing Through

the bathroom and go myself before we got in the car. When I got in the car, I said, "What is wrong with you coming up here to the movie theater?" She said she thought I was there with someone else. I said, "Clearly, I am up here with someone; the baby."

She said, "I wanted to take you guys somewhere today."

I said, "Why didn't you tell me earlier that you wanted to see her?"

She said, "I just decided I wanted to spend time with her."

I told her that I would not be at her beck and call; it's not fair.

Tiny took us to a local department store and we both bought the baby a few outfits. Once back in the car, we passed a restaurant and I told her that I would treat her to dinner. We sat at dinner and all the people walking by admired how beautiful the baby was. We laughed. We ended up having a good conversation. Tiny and I talked about the changes we both needed to make to co-parent, build a friendship, and possibly have a better relationship moving forward. I laughed at her because the list she gave me had fifty things on it and hers only had ten. When she dropped the baby and me off, she asked if she could see the baby on Saturday. I agreed. I asked what time she was coming, and she said 10:00 a.m. I told her fine, and that I would cook breakfast since I hadn't cooked breakfast for us in a while. I texted her early the next morning to let her know that the basement door was unlocked. I asked her what time she was coming so I knew what time to make breakfast, and she said she was on her way. Tiny arrived when my cousin was there visiting the baby and dropping off some new clothes she bought for her. Once my cousin left, Tiny asked if we could go to Atlantic City for the night for some family time. I told her yes. I had a free room on my account with an online hotel site. I looked up the rooms, but they weren't at nice motels. I wanted to book something different, so the online site gave me a credit and I paid the remaining balance. Then it started pouring down rain. We couldn't back out after the room was paid for because check-in was in a few hours. We ran and got dressed, grabbed everything we needed for us and the baby, and headed downtown to the bus station. Tiny paid for our bus tickets and got us some drinks. We had a pleasant conversation on the trip. I talked to her and told her things I've never told her before, and she listened to me. It was nice. We arrived in Atlantic City and played in the casino for a bit. Then Tiny purchased some food for us to take to our room. I paid for a cab to get to our hotel as it had started pouring down raining again. Once we arrived in the room, Tiny played with the baby, and then we ate and talked some more. We had breakfast the next morning and left shortly after checking out. We were on our way to Sassy's house for a Labor Day seafood feast.

Right before we left my house to attend the feast, the baby started screaming again. Tiny asked me what was wrong, and I told her that this was something she had been doing for a while now. Every single time she pooped, she screamed. It's hard for her to poop. She's not constipated, but she strained each time. It had been something that had been breaking my heart for a while, and I just prayed that she'd get through this phase quickly. I'd taken videos of her

Pushing Through

doing it and even wanted to send them to Tiny, but those were days that I was angry that she wasn't there to see the things she went through as a baby. She also had acid reflux, which is why she threw up every single time she fed. It made me sad and depressed seeing her like that because she was usually a very happy baby. To see her in pain hurt me. We put the baby in the car so we could make it in time for the feast, but she was still in the process of pooping. Once we arrived at Sassy's house, we changed her in Sassy's bedroom. We then ate some barbeque, sat around, and talked. I asked Tiny how her moving process was going. She told me she had no intention of moving into her own place. She wanted to give me some time to move back home in two or three months. She asked about a conversation we had when we were together. We had talked about moving out of the state. She asked if would I consider moving out of state with her, and I told her that if she wanted me to move with her that I would. I told her my only hesitation was that my family, friends, and businesses were here in my hometown, and I've lived here all my life. She said we would work that out eventually. I told her that we would revisit the conversation soon, but right then wasn't the time since we hadn't agreed on therapy together or worked on any issues we had, past or present.

We arrived home and put things away and got ready for bed. She told me that I needed to stop holding her to what happened in the past. I told her that I couldn't get over things just like that. It was easy for her to get over things, but I needed to see that the past was not still relevant here in our present. The conversation got heated, so I told her I wanted to do something we had never done before and that was to excuse myself for a minute. She finally agreed.

Charise Marie

I would have normally just walked away and slammed a door, and she would have said that I was ignoring her or running from the argument. This time, however, I went in the bathroom and counted to ten a few times to keep calm. I came back in the room and we argued again because we weren't seeing eye to eye.

We woke up on Labor Day and I made breakfast. I was going to try not to do the things I did before that she didn't like, which, in this case, was bring the argument from the night before into the next day. I clearly would not have made breakfast if I wasn't trying something different. I would have been petty and told her to fix some cereal or oatmeal. She thanked me for breakfast and helped me prepare for the game night that I was having with a bunch of our friends. I told her that I wanted to be clear that the friends she hung out with were no longer my friends. I wanted her to know that if we got back together, we would be separated when it came to the different sets of friends. She started screaming that I was a bad friend because her friends didn't do anything to me. I said it's really not a conversation that we needed to have, but she needed to know that if we got back together, we would have separate friends and spend separate time with them. I told her that I knew she had been telling people lies about me and that is why they acted a certain way toward me. She told me that she'd told the truth the entire time. I said, "I already know the top three things you tell people so they can say 'aw, poor you.' One is that I broke up with you and put you out. Two is that I ran after you with weapons trying to harm you. Three is that I took the baby from you. Yes, I did do one out of those three things, but I never tried to harm you nor did any weapon come near you. And I never tried to take the baby

Pushing Through

from you. You told me you were calling my bluff by leaving. If I tried breaking up with you and told you to get out 8,236 times in seven years and you never left, why would you leave now that we have a baby? I would think that this would be the time where you would pull me aside and say that we both need to stop our shit and do what's best for the baby. If in the end we don't work out but we were doing the work that needed to be done, then yes, I would agree that we break up."

She said, "Well, I felt that you needed time away for two to three months in order to miss what you have."

I said, "This shit is not a game."

She started screaming at me, so I took the baby and walked up the steps. She followed me, and I told her that we didn't have to scream around the baby. She contacted Sassy on the phone and told her that I needed to let go of the past and a whole lot of other things. Sassy told her that we both needed to let go of the past, and to make sure it's buried. Sassy said, "You can't honestly think that Charise will get over anything that's still around. You need to get a new therapist and work on a better plan." Tiny told her no, that she would not get rid of the things that hurt me in the past, and we would not be paying $150 per session for a new therapist when we have a free one. Sassy told her that she thought we needed to find a new therapist who worked solely on our issues, and not someone who dismissed me while knowing I was dealing with postpartum depression. That's not cool. All kinds of things can happen when your hormones are all over the place. She felt that dumping me wasn't cool for a therapist to do.

Charise Marie

Tiny sent me a text the next morning thanking me for the whole weekend and asking me to tell the baby that she loves her. She then texted me to say that our couple's therapist didn't get fired, and I should set up a new appointment with her. That was the story she was trying to tell me anyway, instead of just admitting that she had been petty by dismissing me from therapy. I just told her, "No thank you, I have my therapist." She asked if she could see the baby in two days, and I told her to check in with me on that day since I was having a rough day. She asked if I wanted to talk about it, and I just said no. She said that we had just talked with one another all weekend, but she hoped I felt better. I just told her thanks and to enjoy the rest of her day. The next day she said that she hoped the baby and I were doing well, and that we both needed to keep in touch and check on one another. She said she didn't feel well, and she's praying for us to be a family again. I responded to let her know that the baby had had a bad day and night, so I was praying that the baby felt better and I was excited because she was two months old that day. I later sent her some pictures of the baby all dressed up for her two-month pictures that I took at home. Tiny texted and asked if we could bake her a cake and sing for her for when she turned three months old, and I said yes and laughed.

On Friday afternoon, we went to see an R-rated movie that had just come out. It was based on a book that I read when I was a teenager. Once we arrived home, I asked Tiny what exactly was "family time," and what were we really doing? I was starting to get annoyed, so I told Tiny that her idea of family time was stupid to me. We had gone to dinner, the movies, and casinos together since the baby had been born. She used the words "family time" as a way

Pushing Through

to spend time with the baby. But how were those activities spending time with the baby? I wanted to be left out of the equation; I wanted to continue focusing on getting my health together and stop thinking that we were still together. The only plan was for her to spend time with the baby. These were all places we shouldn't take a baby. I just went along with it to show her that I was not with anyone else, and I eventually wanted our family to work out. I swear I was so confused. My emotions were really getting the best of me. Tiny kept saying that I was clueless and I never comprehended anything. I told her that it was time for her to go because I hated when she said that I never comprehended anything like I was dumb. She later sent me a four-page text message. She said us breaking up was already hard enough to deal with. She said she understood that it was easy for me to pick up and move on quickly. I must be enjoying my single life now, and I must be happy with someone else. She said now is not the time for us to have any more secrets between us because that's what hurt us the whole relationship. She said she wanted us to learn how to have fun and talk to each other without bringing up the main issue that killed our relationship. She said she wished we could erase the past and wished that I would love her like I loved her in the beginning. She said no matter how hurt she was or has been, she would always love me. She said that I question everything she does and think she lies all the time; it makes her feel like I hate her. She said she was willing to go to parenting classes for the baby. She said all she wanted to do was get to know me as a friend so she would know how to love and treat me as a mate. She told me to enjoy my time with my new lover tomorrow because I kept choosing people over her. I texted her the next morning to say that I was sorry that me asking what "family time" was had escalated into an argument. It was not my intention.

I finally had a chance to visit my uncle and aunt at their home. My mom and I surprised my uncle with the baby. They both saw pictures of the baby on social media, but that was it. My uncle asked what was going on with me and Tiny, and I told him that we needed time and space to heal from a lot of stuff. I was dealing with a lot right then: the anniversary of the death of the twins and the PTSD that followed their death, the baby being born and the possibility that I may have PPD, the pain from the C-section, me not working and being the breadwinner of the family, and the breakup between Tiny and me. He said, "I know that's a lot, but just pray on it. If you can talk it out, try to do that calmly. Do you love her?" I told him yes, and he said, "Well, you've got to fight for love sometimes, even when you or she may be wrong. If the relationship is what you want, you've got to make it right if you love her and she loves you."

The baby had an appointment and Tiny had to work, so I scheduled her appointment as late as I could. The doctor asked me to fill out this ten-question questionnaire on her computer as honestly as possible. She told me that the baby would be getting her two-month shots that day. Tiny and I texted back and forth so she knew what floor I was on and I knew when she arrived so I could go open the door for her to come to the baby's room. When we both got back to the room, I gave Tiny the baby and the social worker came in. She said that the test I just took showed that I had scored high for having postpartum depression. I told her I figured that was what the test was about and that quite a few of my

Pushing Through

friends had expressed to me nicely, and some not so nicely, that it sounded like I was suffering from PPD. She asked if she could give me some paperwork and set me up with an appointment to see a therapist, but I told her I already had one.

The baby received her first set of shots and I think both Tiny and I had a tear come out of our eyes seeing her cry in pain like that. Tiny visited with the baby once she took us home. While there, she found out that I had bought two tickets to a play and was giving the other ticket to Sassy. She said, "You know that's something we've always done together. Why did you give her my ticket?" I told her that we were no longer together so why should I take her to a play? She asked me if the theater still had tickets left, and I said yes. She asked if I could get her a ticket near where we were sitting, and it just so happened that I found a ticket right behind Sassy and me. She told me she would give me the money later, and I said okay. She later texted me saying that today had been a good day because we had had a nice calm conversation, but she was sad about the baby needles. She said she was praying for more peaceful days to come.

I later posted the following on social media:

When your daughters doctor gives you a 10-question computerized questionnaire to fill out & the social worker walks in to say your score indicates you have Postpartum Depression. When you go to your first doctor's appointment to see if you have it & they say you do have Postpartum Depression, let's make a plan. When some of your friends recognized some of your symptoms being Postpartum Depression and nicely tell you We Got U & Baby Girl,

Charise Marie

Gods Got You & Baby Girl's back & We Are Here for Both of You. Keep these REAL GOOD friends. I never asked to lose my twins & my tubes at the same damn time. I never asked to have Post Traumatic Stress Disorder(PTSD) after the loss of my twins. I never asked for my Relatives to turn other family members against me because I lost my twins & couldn't answer the phone while away on my anniversary trip in the Bahamas with Tiny. I never asked for my female relative to follow in their footsteps & turn against me & spread vicious rumors about me. I never asked for people who said they were "friends" to turn against me. I never asked to be screamed at or made to look crazy because I didn't know what was wrong with me. I never asked to have Postpartum Depression after the birth of my daughter. I never asked for my pressure to be sky high because I'm trying to continuously fight through all of this. I did ask God to help me have another child. Now I'm asking God to help me because I'm dealing with 2 sets of Depression at the same damn time. I don't say this for pity at all. I say it because this shit is real.

    Some nights when Tiny and I talked or texted, I showed her how to do the video chat on social media so she could see the baby on the days she didn't come to visit her. She enjoyed seeing the baby, and we both enjoyed the conversations that we were having. It was refreshing that we could do something we barely did during our entire relationship: talk calmly to one another. She changed her day to see the baby from Tuesday to Wednesday that week, so Sassy wanted to get me out of the house because she said I needed some fresh air. We did some shopping, and then she treated me to the movies. I told her that I was so stressed out that I had stopped producing breast milk. I got teary eyed because

Pushing Through

I wanted to breastfeed the baby, but because I wasn't eating right, and my stress level was so high, my breast milk just stopped completely. She said she figured it would stop soon because every time she checked on me to see if I was eating, I told her that I had had Pepsi and snacks or little things in between.

Tiny texted me because she saw that I was on social media when I told her I was at the movie theater. She said she was going to work on the way she felt because she was having a hard time believing I was at the movies, but she was just expressing her thoughts to me. She said she still thought we were together sometimes, and our breakup was hard, and that's why she's always comparing things we did in the past to now. She said she's going to keep praying to learn how to get through things separately. She's also going to keep me and our little family in prayer.

She came by the next day and started saying that she wanted unsupervised visits with the baby. I knew by this point that one of her friends put this idea in her head. Other times when I asked her if she wanted to be around the baby by herself, she told me no because she didn't know how to do some things like strap her in the car seat correctly or change her diaper on her lap. I told her that I needed to file for full custody to make sure no one tried to take my baby away from me. She got mad at me and started screaming. I asked her to lower her voice, and she told me no because I was pissing her off. I then said that this was why I didn't want her around my baby because she felt it necessary to scream around her. She clearly didn't care anything about her. Didn't she know that she could make her nerves bad doing that? I said, "Plus, you felt it necessary to leave her

Charise Marie

when she was sick, so you don't care now, so get out." She grabbed the ticket I got her for the play and stormed out the house crying and saying that I was being petty, and that if I didn't want her in my or the baby's lives, then she would be gone for good. She later sent me another long text message saying what I said to her was messed up, and she never believed I went to the movies anyway. She said that this was the last time I would intentionally hurt her and push her away. She said she never asked for the breakup, and it's sad that the baby is pulled into our mess. She said that I needed to stop listening to people and letting them win by ending our relationship and not working on it. She said she had been praying on our situation and had given it to God. I should be happy that she wanted to raise the baby with me. She said she felt powerless in this whole situation because I controlled everything.

    I just let things die down for a few days because my blood pressure kept getting higher and higher. My friends and family were very concerned. My therapist felt it was best that I stayed as calm as possible, especially since I had post traumatic stress disorder and postpartum depression. They felt it was too much for me to handle. My friends and family were the ones who heard me crying and frustrated over everything that was going on. My family members didn't want to believe I had postpartum depression. Depression, suicide and mental illness are not usually talked about in African-American families. If you were to bring up any of these topics, the response would be "Hush, girl" or "Are you crazy?"

    Days went by and I just kept thinking about how I hadn't had a lot of time to just reflect on the new life I had with a

Pushing Through

baby and no partner by my side. We had a bowling fundraiser for the non-profit organization I started, and Tiny was still a part of it. I brought her the mail and asked her if she wanted to hold the baby, and she said yes. I asked her when was she going to give me the money for the play ticket, and she said she thought I was taking her to make up for all I'd done to her. I just laughed, and said, "Whatever, keep the money." I felt like saying, "You have three jobs, two of which came from my family members so you could help me with our household expenses while we were living together, and I'm on unemployment, and you can't give me the money?" But this wasn't the place to have that conversation. Plus, I didn't feel like arguing and being called petty again.

We continued to text each other saying things like "thanks for the good conversation" or "thanks for checking on me." I still sent her pictures and videos of the baby. She texted me to see if I wanted a ride to the play, and I told that I would meet her there. She told me to stop changing plans and that she was going to take me and that was that. Then she quickly realized that she no longer was fussing with me, and I could ride with the person who was taking me. She said that she wanted to see the baby before I dropped her off, and that she wished our communication was better. We talked on the phone later. I explained to her that I was going to take a cab because I didn't need her accusing me of needing her to take me anywhere. I told her it's funny that she kept accusing me of being with other people. How did I know she wasn't with someone? I said, "I keep hearing that you're out courting someone, so stop trying to make it look like it's me."

Tiny ended up picking me up from my mom's house,

where I dropped off the baby, and we had a relatively calm conversation in the car. We enjoyed the play, and she later texted me thanking me for the night out. She wanted me to look up tickets for one of the local young adults concerts they have in our city. I told her that she was welcome for the play, that I would look up the tickets, and to have a good night.

That weekend was the couple's game night that I had planned at the hotel. Tiny told me that she still wanted to be a part of it like every other time I had done it in the past. I told her that we were together then and we always stayed in the hotel. I told her that I thought she only wanted to help me because she thought someone was staying with me in the hotel room I booked. She asked if she could come pick me up to get the last-minute items for the game night, and I finally agreed. When we came back in the house to finish cooking, she asked if I would move in with her if I didn't sell my house. I told her I might. She didn't like that answer, so I changed it to yes. She asked if I ever looked up the tickets for the concert, and I said I had forgotten. She asked if I really wanted to go, and I kept beating around the bush because I was at the point of wanting to completely distance myself from her. Things were still up and down with us, and my mind was racing. I then told her that I would go with her to the concert. She gave me her debit card, and I ordered two tickets over the phone for us.

We left for the hotel and the game night was really nice. All those who attended my third-annual game night said they enjoyed themselves. But Tiny and I immediately started arguing once everyone left. We both sat there in the hotel room crying, frustrated, and just angry. I accused her

Pushing Through

of seeing someone; she accused me. I told her she didn't care about me or the baby; she said I didn't care about her. This went on for two hours. I got up to grab something to drink and realized how much pain I was in when I tried to walk across the room. She asked what was wrong, and I told her that standing on my legs for game night for that long period of time hurt. Tiny grabbed her rubbing alcohol and rubbed my legs down. I thanked her. We had breakfast the next morning in the hotel before we packed up and left. We had a long, calm conversation trying to figure out what to do. We agreed to have better communication, to leave the past in the past, and not to bring up anything that could cause an argument. I told her I didn't know how to let go, but that I had to find some way to move on and stop feeling hurt over everything from the past. I then told Tiny that the fertility clinic contacted me about the one embryo I had left because if I decided to keep it they would start charging me for storage for the next year. She asked if I was going to have this next baby for her, and I looked at her and laughed. She asked what was so funny, and I told her that I had to get over the fact that I felt like she abandoned me and the baby as soon as I started dealing with postpartum and the baby had tummy issues. Tiny kept telling me that she wanted me to do all these things to change, and I told her that I was willing to make changes, but that I couldn't be the only one making changes just for us to go back to the way our relationship was. We both finally agreed on going to counseling together.

For a while it was always one of us that wanted to go to therapy, then the other one. Never both of us at the same time. This went on for weeks. She had time off from work at the beginning of October and asked if I wanted to spend

Charise Marie

those few days in Atlantic City. I agreed. I booked our room for that Sunday night and she booked it for that Monday night.

A few days later, I decided to do something I thought I would never be able to accomplish: a Suicide Awareness Walk. My legs were in severe pain from the walk because of my surgery as a kid, but I had wanted to do something that was relevant in my life. I almost took my life a few times when I lost my twins. I was amazed by all the people who walked and had on shirts from loved ones they lost to suicide. I thought, Wow! This would be my family and friends if I had taken my life three years ago. My friend Kelly walked with me and I truly appreciated it. We walked under the name of my non-profit organization, Great Services Association. Tiny texted me and asked how was the walk and I just told her it went well. I was physically and emotionally drained so I didn't really want to talk to her.

Tiny asked me the next day to write her a letter expressing my feeling about her openly and honestly. She said I should include things I had wanted to say but never said, or how I'd felt about things that I'd never expressed. She knew that over the years I stopped expressing my feelings to her because I told her I felt like every time I talked to her it felt like she dismissed my feelings. So, I sat down and wrote her a twenty-six-page letter on everything I could think of: my weight loss, ignorant or rude comments, lies, infidelity, my self-esteem, kids, family, friends, and so much more. I told her I never knew how I truly felt about her. My feelings surfaced only after being hurt so much in the relationship I felt like she didn't love me, so I suppressed my feelings for her. My emotions came flooding back ever since I had the baby

Pushing Through

and our breakup. I told her that I cried every night because I missed her, but that I couldn't go back to the hurt and pain we caused each other. My therapist told me that she didn't want me to repeat any of the behavior I had in the beginning with the weapons or even the suicidal attempts. I also wrote to her that I felt like we were still in a relationship, and I was tired of the back and forth and the arguing. It felt like we were still playing games with one another, and I was just tired. The therapist told me I needed to let her go until I was in a better place mentally and emotionally, and to find a way for her to co-parent without me having to be around her while she visited the baby. I had told the therapist about the previous arguments, and she said letting go would best for my healing. I would never heal properly if I continued to argue and keep her around.

Tiny texted me to ask why I hadn't sent any pictures, videos, or good morning messages to her the next week. I texted her back and told her that I didn't mean any harm, but that I was suffering through some rough moments in my life, and I know she loves the baby, but my doctor thought it best that I step back from her for a little while and that included the baby as well. I needed some time to get myself together, and I hoped she'd understand. Once I felt like myself again, I would contact her to see the baby. I told her that I wouldn't be able to go to Atlantic City or the concert. She responded saying she was pissed off with me playing games with her and that she didn't believe that my therapist gave me this advice but it was my friends who told me instead. She said, "I'm going to grant you your wish since you don't want me in your life or the baby's. It's always your rules, and it's unfair that you are being selfish." I called Sassy, cried on the phone, and told her what Tiny

Charise Marie

had said to me. I said, "Why am I wrong for wanting to get myself together? I just need a little bit of time for my blood pressure to come down and for me to stop sitting around hoping that if I hurt myself she will come running back to tell me she loves me, and say 'Babe it's going to be alright; I'm here for you.'" Then I thought, if I did hurt myself, would she come running? I shouldn't have to feel that me getting the help I need is wrong. I was so angry that she said that. Sassy told me to just do what my therapist said was best and to pray on it. I told her that I wanted to be alright for the baby. I'd read all kinds of stories about women hurting themselves, their partners, or their kids because of suffering from postpartum depression, and I didn't want to be one of them. Even though I could never and would never harm my daughter, I didn't want to harm myself thinking Tiny would come running to see if I was okay.

    I didn't get it. I'd never dealt with this before: a breakup on top of post traumatic stress disorder and postpartum depression. This shit hurt like hell, and I didn't know what to do. Should I have told her I still wanted to go and kept on trying to work it out with her? I felt like she didn't care about my depression. I was tired of crying. I'd never cried this much in my life. I said it didn't matter because she cared nothing about me and never loved me even after seven years. Sassy said, "You will be fine. You'll do what's best for you and the baby. You have to find a way to get through this like the therapist said, because at the end of the day, who will take care of you? You have to take care of you. You can't expect everyone to care for you like you do yourself. It's going to be just fine because you have family and friends who love you and who will see you through this rough time. Just stay calm and make sure you keep taking

Pushing Through

your blood pressure medications and eat something." I thanked her and wiped my tears. I was on the train going home and I had never cried like that in public. I was so glad to have Sassy in my life. We were pretty good friends before, but after the breakup she had been there for me every day to make sure the baby was fine, and that I was okay and taking my medication and eating.

I contacted a ton of friends and told them I needed to get out on Friday night to dance, drink, and have a good time. I needed to have some fun, and I heard my favorite exotic dancer would be at a local strip club. They all came out and I had a VIP section already set for us. We arrived, and I saw Tiny sitting with Irene and Nic, the two she called every single time we argued about something. I went over and spoke to all of them and they spoke back. I got a round of drinks for all my friends and thanked them for coming out and enjoying the night with me.

Normally, I turned my phone on silent every night so it wouldn't disturb the baby or me while we're sleeping. Sunday morning at 1:52, I heard the text message sound and was startled. I had forgotten to turn the sound off because I had been super tired. It was Tiny. She said, "I pay attention to everything you do. I know you lied last week, and instead of you telling me you're messing around with someone and have moved on with your life, you lied about needing space like your doctor said." She then went on to say that I treated her like she meant nothing to me for seven years. I didn't wear jewelry and make up when I was with her, but I did at the club and all the time now without her. She said she wasn't going to beg to see the baby anymore and would always keep the baby and me in prayer. I was so floored by

Charise Marie

her three-page text message that I ran in the bathroom, away from the baby, and called her three times. She didn't pick up. I immediately started crying and trying to figure out what to do. I texted her back and said that I didn't understand what I did to her that was so wrong to cause her to hate me so much. I'd been stressing and crying every day, and she kept assuming I was with someone else when I was so messed up over her. My doctor knew that I had a history of suicidal thoughts and thought I needed time to get myself to heal before anything happened. I texted, "Now I'm sitting in the bathroom crying because you seem not to care about my depression because you think I'm with someone else. I wore all those things for you and have pictures to prove it; you just didn't pay any attention to me. I'm not the one talking to someone else. People always say it's the person who accuses the other who is really guilty, so stop saying it's me. The people in my life care about my well-being and for my daughter. All I've asked you for since this breakup is intense therapy for us to get through the past issues we had, but clearly, I still see things will always be about you. When was the last time you asked me about how I was doing or if I was okay?" She then called me at 2:54 a.m., right after texting me, and we were on the phone until 10:04 a.m. Yes, seven hours. Most of the call drained the life out of me and I just couldn't understand what was going on. I kept crying because she just didn't get how I was feeling or seem to care about it. She asked me if I would be by her side when she got an upcoming surgery, even after everything we'd been through and me feeling like she didn't care about me or the baby. I told her yes. She said that we needed to communicate better and fix us the right way. She had tried planning things for us to do, family things for the three of us, and building a better friendship between us,

Pushing Through

but I was negative like I was all the time. We only broke up because I ended the relationship because I'm always angry even though we both messed up. She said that I never believed anything she said, and that I kept telling myself that she didn't care about me and other negative things. If she didn't care, she would have not been trying to do things together as a family. If I would have waited and been patient enough, I would have seen how she would have been able to support me through all the things I was going through. She hoped the Lord would show me one day that my negative thinking was wrong, and that I pushed her away when she really did care. Tiny then said that the things I said to her in the letter didn't match up, because one minute I said one thing, and the next minute I said something else. If I wanted her, I would stop pushing her away. She had tried many different attempts to fix our relationship such as the concert and us going away for a few days with the baby, but I didn't see that. She felt like I was playing games with her because I said one day she could see the baby and the next she couldn't. She had no issue with getting to know what was going on with me. She said she could have gone to one of my therapy sessions to know how to interact with me.

    She finally asked me what was going on with me, and I told her that when we were at the baby's doctor appointment, the social worker said I had postpartum depression. She said she didn't recall her saying that. I told her that my doctor diagnosed me with having it a week later. She said she also didn't understand why I kept saying it's called "postpartum depression" when everything she looked up on the internet didn't say "depression," so I should stop saying I'm depressed and adding depression to it because it doesn't sound good. She then asked me what it was like for

Charise Marie

me dealing with postpartum. I told her that some days I was happy, some days I was sad, some days I cried, some days I was perfectly fine, some days I hated her, and on other days I loved her. I even told her that one day I had wanted to hurt myself in hopes that she would come back and understand what was going on with me. I wanted her to show me that she loved me and only wanted me and the baby. I told her every day was different for me. She asked if I was serious about hurting myself, and I told her yeah, but I had called a friend and she told me to focus and pray because that was not what I should be wanting to do. I told that friend that I was having a moment, but I thanked her for listening to me. I told her that I even was upset when her friend criticized me for sitting in the back seat with the baby every time we were in the car. She said I acted like something was going to happen to the baby if she sat in the back alone. I told her I was upset she laughed at the friend's comment and agreed like I was being foolish sitting back there. Tiny said that I would see one day how I feed my head with silly stuff and how I let other people feed my head with silly stuff when I should have paid attention to her attempting to show that she cared about me. When she finally agreed to therapy months later, I should have noticed it because that was her way of showing she cared. She told me she was going to take some time and get herself together. Focus on her health and getting a new place. She said she didn't want to be in a relationship right now until she has her heart clear from loving me in order to be right for the next woman. Tiny said that included being with me, someone new or going back to someone from her past. She said I would be the one to hop in a relationship before she did and I explained to her my focus is for me to get better first. Getting out of one relationship into the next was not my focus.

Pushing Through

Before we got off the phone, we agreed to meet downtown because our city was having a big gay festival. I told her I was meeting up with one of our mutual friends, and she got mad because the girl was a tomboy. I just said to stop being foolish because we just had a good ending to this seven-hour conversation. Please chill out. Once I arrived down there, I walked around, but it was too humid out so I was ready to go. I called Tiny and she told me where she was located. Once we met up, she kissed the baby, we hugged each other, and we talked for twenty minutes. She then checked her phone and said that Irene and Nic were on their way. I got pissed off because the way she said it to me was like she was dismissing me and like she didn't want them to see us together, so I stormed off. She called me back to her and we argued. I told her that I wouldn't argue with her in public so to enjoy the day and go hang with her friends.

    Later, I learned about the lies that were being told about me. I was devastated and hurt. I contacted my close girlfriend and she asked me if what was being said was true, and could the source who told me be trusted? I told her what was said matched up to things that happened between Tiny and me. I said I could imagine the things being said about me to other people who didn't even know me, and I started to cry. I told my friend that I was going to block all communication from Tiny, so she couldn't call me, text me, or even contact me via social media. I told her I wasn't just blocking her based on what was said, but that I had to get myself together. I was dealing with a lot, and me getting better was not going to work if I had to keep dealing with the same stuff. I said that I kept telling Tiny that I knew she was lying about me, but to hear it confirmed was what really hurt. What devastated me the most was more

Charise Marie

than one person stating the same comment made about my daughter. I cried when I heard more than one person make this same specific comment to me. No matter what the circumstances, I felt alone and like my postpartum depression wasn't being supported. It was like a joke. Not only to her but other people as well. It felt like my postpartum depression magnified my situation even more. I walked around crying because I felt like I shouldn't be in this situation, but with the grace of God and good people in my life, I realized that things happen for a reason and that I will get through it. My friend just couldn't believe what I was telling her. She said that I had to do what's best for me first in order for the baby to be good too. I told her that if this means that I'm sacrificing my relationship with Tiny for my health to be good then I have to take that risk. They say if it's meant to be it will be and come back to you. Only time will be able to tell that. Tiny and I have not spoken since the day after I saw her. She hasn't participated in any of the volunteering activities put on by my non-profit organization, nor has she seen or asked about the baby since that day.

Pushing Through

"Be the change that you wish to see in the world."

- Mahatma Gandhi

Charise Marie

Chapter Twelve: After the Storm, There's a Rainbow

I went to the hospital a few months back because I felt as if my head was about to burst. I knew it was my high blood pressure. I felt my pressure going up for a long time, and I had been trying to get it down for weeks. On some days my mother and son took my daughter so I could get a little bit of rest or relaxation to try and bring it down. On this particular day, I arrived at the hospital and they told me my blood pressure was 164/79. They gave me an IV to try and flush out whatever was in my system. They also gave me painkillers because they said I may have a severe migraine. By the time I was getting ready to leave, my pressure was 183/95 and the nurse looked at me. I told the nurse that she needed to get a doctor, but they ended up releasing me. I was told to take things slow and easy. I knew from that day that I did not want to jeopardize my health in any way, and I didn't care who didn't like it. If something happens to me, who will take care of my daughter?

I decided to finally take my driver's permit test. I had a huge run around as the DMV said my paperwork wasn't clear because the doctor didn't fill it out correctly. It wasn't legible, and it was missing some information. So, I ran around stalking the doctor's office until they completed it correctly. I studied the permit test on an app on my phone for a very long time. I had tried to get my permit when I was pregnant because I had some time off, but I didn't feel

Pushing Through

comfortable going to the DMV by myself since I always felt faint. I didn't want to pass out there by myself. In October, I took my permit test and passed on the first try. I was ecstatic. I scheduled my driving lessons immediately after passing the test. I did approximately five sessions. The day of my driving test, I failed. The instructor said it was because of my turns, which was what I had struggled with during my lessons. So, we focused on that more when I booked extra lessons. I didn't care how much money I spent on lessons, I wanted to be able to drive correctly. My driving instructor told me the morning of my next test that I did great. I think the tester had a bad lunch before he saw me, because I thought I did well but he failed me. He said it was because of my turns being too narrow and my steering. I scheduled my next test as soon as I left the testing center. I was sad about failing for a few minutes, but my friends and family told me to hold up my chin; I'd pass my next test. I will get my driver's license! I was determined! The second day of the new year I went in for my next driving test and passed my driver's test! I was elated! I purchased my very first car the next day. What a great way to start off the new year after having a rough year last year.

One of the many other things I'm focusing on moving forward in my life is expanding my non-profit organization, Great Services Association. I want to buy a building and have sponsors donate things for us to give to the less fortunate in a poor area in the community. I want to be able to provide things they are unable to provide for themselves. I'm in the process of working with a few people to help me make this dream come true. We have a large list of things we would like to provide to the community.

Charise Marie

I had to take off a year from college myself because of the threatened miscarriage I suffered, and I could not focus on anything at that time. I told the college a few weeks after the baby was born that I would be back. The next thing I knew, I was going through a breakup and postpartum depression. So, I took off the entire year because I knew I would not be able to focus on anything other than me and the baby. The college reached out to me and asked if I was coming back, and I told them I would be back at the beginning of this year. I am determined to get my degree in Business Management.

I never thought in a million years I would be where I am today. I'm a mother again for the third time; technically my second time. It feels so good too. Looking at my baby growing and smiling every day brightens up my day. When she laughs when she's awake and in her sleep, it warms my heart. She's eating puréed foods that I make for her at home, and I love feeding her, holding her, spending time with her, and loving her. Sometimes it's all about the little things, like when her little hand grabs the side of my face, I just melt. Bath time with her is so much fun she laughs the entire time. Even dressing and undressing her she giggles and it's so cute. Was I sleep deprived when she first was born? I certainly was, but I got up and did exactly what a mother is supposed to do every single day. I laugh every time when someone asks me how many kids I have and I say two kids. Once I give their ages and people hear that they are almost 19 years apart people are shocked. I then tell some of them my story and they understand but still think I'm crazy for having kids so far apart in age.

We are super blessed because the baby still receives gifts

Pushing Through

from people on my social media page; people I have never met but who have watched and followed me and my journeys for years. It warms my heart to know that these people care. Some of these people heard my cries via social media talking about my struggles with the loss of income. It feels good when people love and care so much about you.

    I questioned God for a very long time, especially when I was angry. Sometimes we have to stop questioning and just accept things for what they are. God answers prayers in his time. I had to learn to be patient. You just have to believe things will work out in the end.

    I've had to learn ways of forgiving and letting go. Friends, family members, and therapists had given me suggestions over the years, but they just never worked for me. Ever! A few friends told me to get a book and write my feelings and the things that I could not forgive or let go down. Others told me that I should write it down and burn it. I started writing things down to try and release it. Now I'm at a point in my life where if things aren't good for me, I just say I'm letting that go, I forgive you; and I do just that: let it go. People always say that forgiveness isn't about the other person, it's about you, but this theory never worked for me. I guess what I did most of the time was sweep things under the rug; but they were always there. My ex Tiny and I had breakfast one morning at a new diner just before our breakup, and she asked me why forgiveness never worked for me. What did I do to get through things, or did they come up day by day? I gave her an example of what and how my thinking works. I told her to think of it this way: There's a brick lying in front of you, and you step over this brick every single day because you know the brick is there. Technically, it's always in the back of your mind. You're used to stepping over it, but you know it's always there. Every day you leave for work, school, or shopping, and each day you continue to step over this brick. One day as you are leaving in a rush, you forget that the brick is there, and you stumble over it. You're mad that you messed up your new shoes or ripped your stockings. Now you're thinking about all the other times you stumbled over the brick and fell or messed up something. She said, "Okay, I get it." I explained that that brick is the past. It's always there. What do you think you should do? Sometimes you're so used to moving on with life that you pay no attention to it until one day, boom! It hits you dead smack in your face. My problem is that I've never moved the brick; I never knew how to so I just kept stepping over it. For me, it wasn't as simple as picking it up and moving it. She said, "That's deep." I said that my analogy might not make sense to her but that's my thinking. I said you know my thinking is a little different because of my dyslexia.

    What's crazy to me is that people have said that I'm an inspiration to them. I am in awe and denial when I hear it most times. They send me messages via social media, telling me that I helped them lose weight, make a decision about a friend or family member, start a new business, and even get pregnant. My mouth is on the floor usually as I'm just an ordinary girl who has gone through things in life that I was able to overcome or push through. Most people surprised me so much with the "Thank You" or "You are such an inspiration" messages that I would look in the mirror and wonder who they were talking to. I struggle daily with many different things, but I'm always able to help someone else. I'm a work in progress: God's beautiful art

Pushing Through

project. He's not through with me yet, though. He had me go through many things in life, I guess with the hope that I'd help others. Even if I just help one person, I've helped someone.

Every day moving forward, I try to remain positive and focus on the good things that are happening in my life. Some days I fall short, but I pray every time I feel myself drifting to the negative side. I even picked up a positive journal that has five-minute daily activities you can answer to remain positive. Having my faith restored in God again is helping me push through all the things I have going on in my life. I'm excited because, although I was unable to put my son through college because I was financially unable, he will still be able to attend the same college the following year. I was hurt and cried when the admissions office at the college told me that he couldn't attend because I couldn't afford to pay the fees. God willing, he will be in college next summer; I'm going to make sure of it. In the meantime, he is working and is excited to go to college. He told me he understood what happened about the money and didn't blame me for it. I'm extra excited that even though my kids are eighteen years apart, they have the best bond ever. My son spoils the baby by picking her up, playing with her, and playing all kinds of lullabies on his phone for her. He walks in the room and she immediately looks for him. Their bond is so cute. I pray that they stay close in the coming years.

My therapist booked me an appointment to see the psychiatrist to determine whether I needed medication. She said it's routine that I'm evaluated by one. The appoint-

Charise Marie

ment was at the end of the year, and once I finally arrived, the psychiatrist asked several questions. I answered them honestly. The best thing she said was that I didn't need any medication. She said, "I think you need lots of therapy for the things that you have been through, and I see you are doing that, so keep up the good work. I don't want to put you on medication to alter your mind. I think you have a great head on your shoulders and will get through everything you have going on with postpartum depression and anything else just fine. Just focus on all the things you said you are doing and remain positive." I was elated to hear that. I wasn't opposed to taking medication, but I was super happy that I wasn't diagnosed as sick enough to have to take any. I don't knock anyone that has to take medication, but I take enough medication for asthma, migraines, and high blood pressure; I don't need any more added to the list.

I continue to see my therapist every two weeks. She set up a plan for me to remain positive, and to focus on me, the baby, and all the other great things I have planned for my life. She wants me to stay on the right path so I don't fall back into any of the negative behaviors that I displayed in my past. My therapist has been great since day one. She's never judged me or looked at me like I was crazy. Dealing with PTSD and PPD at the same time has had its challenges. The great thing I noticed is that it's not the end of the world. I'm praying that her plan to keep me on a positive path will stay with me the rest of my life. There are great things ahead for me, and, with the grace of God, I will accomplish everything set before me.

I found a saying on social media that said: When God is

Pushing Through

doing some rearranging in your life, don't fight it. Yield to the Lord, and let Him work. The result will be beautiful.

When I started to see that God was shifting my life, I tried to fight it. I couldn't understand it. I kept wanting to change my life to what I thought it should be. I had to finally let him work on me in his own way. He obviously knew what was best for me. I had to learn that lesson back in July 2014, after thinking I had things all planned out for what I wanted and where I wanted my life to go. I also saw this one saying online: If you want to make God laugh, tell him your plans. I did that all the time; I thought I was in control when he was THE only one in control. He knew the path he wanted my life to follow. But I couldn't understand for the life of me why he took me through so much in my life.

When life knocks you down nine times, you get back up that tenth time. Don't let anything keep you down. When the devil is whispering in your ear, "You are not strong enough to withstand this storm", whisper back "I am the storm." They say when life throws you lemons, you make lemonade, right? I tend to make lemonade, lemon pie, lemon candy, lemon cake, etc. One thing in my life I tried never to do was throw the lemon away. I say that to mean, keep pushing through life. Life throws us curve balls all the time. When life gives you a hundred reasons to cry, show life that you have a thousand reasons to smile.

I tell people all the time to keep going, never stop, remain determined, that you can do it, and to just keep pushing through.

Charise Marie

I saw this on social media and thought that it fit great to end my book with this quote.

"I've learned a lot this year. I learned that things don't always turn out the way you planned, or the way you think they should. And I've learned that there are things that go wrong that don't always get fixed or get put back together the way they were before. I've learned that some broken things stay broken, and I've learned that you can get through bad times and keep looking for better ones, as long as you have people who love you." – Jennifer Weiner

About the Author

Charise Marie is a mother, a daughter, a sister, a friend and a child of God. She is the mother of two beautiful children, Mr. J & Ms. Z, as well as two heavenly twin angels. She is currently finishing her degree in Business Management. Charise is an entrepreneur of multiple businesses including her very own non-profit organization. She hopes to have her own non-profit building one day to help serve the less fortunate in the community. She is also now an author of her very first book, "Pushing Through."